THE

skinnytaste
AIR FRYER

COOKBOOK

CLARKSON POTTER/
PUBLISHERS

NEW YORK

THE
skinnytaste
AIR FRYER
COOKBOOK

the 75 BEST HEALTHY RECIPES
for your AIR FRYER

GINA HOMOLKA
WITH HEATHER K. JONES, R.D.

CONTENTS

INTRODUCTION

Yes! You finally bought an air fryer! Perhaps you don't know what to make with it or exactly how to use it. Not to worry. Be prepared to become an air fryer aficionado!

If it weren't for the constant emails from Skinnytaste fans asking me for air fryer recipes, I probably wouldn't have discovered what all the fuss was about. I resisted buying an air fryer for quite a while because I really didn't want another gadget or cooking appliance taking up space in my kitchen. My thought was, *What can the air fryer do that I can't do with my oven?* I admit I was skeptical. The first recipe I tested was my Buttermilk Oven "Fried" Chicken from my first cookbook, *The Skinnytaste Cookbook*. The recipe came out perfectly crispy—golden chicken that was juicy and perfectly cooked on the inside— and in half the time it would have taken in the oven. I was amazed.

I started testing all my fried favorites— french fries, chicken wings, onion rings, breaded chicken cutlets. I was really impressed! Food came out so much crispier than I could achieve in my oven. And many times, I even had my husband fooled that it wasn't fried. Needless to say, I was a convert.

Suddenly it became a fun challenge trying everything I could think of in my new appliance. Roasted vegetables won me over. Charred string beans, roasted Brussels sprouts, and crisp cauliflower came out perfectly browned—exactly the way I love them. Then I started playing around with salmon, lamb chops, burgers, bagels, and even pizza. I was hooked! There are so many positives: The air fryer takes only three minutes to preheat, doesn't heat up the kitchen, is safer and healthier than deep frying, and doesn't smoke up the whole house.

This easy, useful kitchen appliance has now replaced my oven on most weekdays and -nights, whether I'm whipping up a side dish, heating up leftovers, or making supper. In fact, I love it so much that I decided to brand my own and create my first product: the Skinnytaste by Vremi Air Fryer. You may be overwhelmed with the options of air fryer models available on the market, from basket-style (like mine), to toaster oven-style (such as the Cuisinart Air Fryer Toaster Oven or the Breville Smart Oven Air). The good news: All the recipes in this book will work for any model. I've included directions for both styles, and I've added cook times for a conventional oven for those of you who have no desire to purchase an air fryer (see chart on page 155).

There's plenty of air fryer cookbooks out there, but they're not necessarily healthy or light, so I knew a Skinnytaste air fryer cookbook had to be written. Each recipe includes nutrition information as well as a recipe key labeling recipes that are at or under thirty minutes in cook time, vegetarian, gluten-free, dairy-free, keto-friendly, and freezer-friendly.

I hope this book and an air fryer itself will inspire you in the kitchen. Have fun with the appliance, and be prepared to fall in love. I guarantee you'll find ways to use it in everyday cooking.

Recipe Key

Look for these helpful icons throughout the book:

Q Quick (ready in 30 minutes or less)

V Vegetarian

GF Gluten-Free

DF Dairy-Free

K Keto-Friendly

FF Freezer-Friendly

Weight Watchers Points

For those of you on Weight Watchers, all of the up-to-date Weight Watchers Points are conveniently located on my website under the cookbook tab: www.skinnytaste.com/cookbook.

AIR FRYER BASICS

What is an air fryer, anyway? It's basically a countertop convection oven with a heated coil (usually at the top), a mesh or metal basket, and a fan that circulates the heat around the foods at convection oven rates. Cooking food in an oven creates steam, and deep-frying works by flash-cooking foods in hot oil, but the air fryer cooking method creates an efficient, intense environment of heat that consequently cooks foods faster and more evenly. This results in crisp, browned exteriors and juicy, tender interiors. It's much healthier, safer, and cleaner than deep-frying foods, but it doesn't stop there—with an air fryer, you can also roast vegetables and fish, bake muffins and quiche, reheat leftovers, and heat up frozen foods. It basically does the work of an oven, a deep fryer, and a microwave—all in one.

CHOOSING AND USING YOUR FRYER

Air fryers come in different shapes and sizes, from compact cylindrical countertop styles with a fryer basket (and some even have built-in rotisseries) to convection toaster oven–style fryers. Toaster-style air fryers are larger than most basket-style models, so you can cook most recipes in one batch, which is convenient for larger families. The downside to that is they tend to take up more counter space. Basket-style air fryers, on the other hand, are more compact and come in a variety of sizes. If you're cooking for just one or two people, a 3-quart basket-style fryer is perfect. If

you're cooking for a family of three or four, you'll want a model that's at least 5.5 quarts and up.

To get consistent results, preheating the air fryer for three minutes is *key*. If your air fryer doesn't come with a preheat function, before you begin cooking, simply set the air fryer (with the basket inserted) for three minutes to the temperature you plan on using.

Cook times will vary slightly depending on the wattage and brand of your air fryer. All the recipes in this book were tested with the Skinnytaste by Vremi 1,700-watt air fryer and the Cuisinart Air Fryer Toaster Oven. For the best results, get to know your air fryer and make adjustments as needed. And don't be afraid to open the air fryer to check your food—some models will shut off when opened, but they will continue to cook once you close the lid again.

An air fryer is also a great tool for reheating foods, much like a microwave, but without making food rubbery. There are really no rules for reheating food in the air fryer—I usually set the temperature to 400°F and check often on the progress of cooking, until the food is hot.

TIPS FOR FRYER SUCCESS

- **Use olive oil spray.** Even though air fryers can cook without oil, foods that are typically deep-fried or breaded will taste best if they're sprayed with olive oil—and a little goes a long way. For best results, spray both sides of your food with a light spray of olive oil before putting it in the basket. You can purchase an oil mister and fill it with your favorite oil, or you can buy a propellant-free olive oil spray with no additives, such as Bertolli 100% Extra-Virgin Olive Oil Spray.

- **Don't forget to flip.** Since the air fryer heating element is usually at the top, flipping your food halfway is essential for evenly cooked and browned food on both sides. For smaller foods, such as french fries or vegetables, shaking the basket a few times (rather than flipping) will result in everything getting evenly browned and crisp.

- **Don't overcrowd the basket.** Always cook food in a single layer. If an item doesn't fit, cook the food in batches to avoid overcrowding the basket. Overcrowding prevents the air from circulating around the food and keeps it from browning and turning crisp. To ensure food comes out hot and at the same time, once all the food is cooked and browned in batches, you can put it back into the basket and heat it together for one to two minutes.

AIR FRYER ACCESSORIES

Investing in some accessories opens up your possibilities for making more dishes, such as frittatas, small cakes, skewers, casseroles, and more! Chances are, you may already have some: Any oven-safe baking dish or cake pan that fits in the air fryer without coming into contact with the heating element will work. Disposable mini foil pie pans and cupcake liners are also great for baking.

CONVERTING RECIPES TO YOUR FRYER

For traditional oven-baked recipes, you can convert them for the air fryer by reducing the temperature by 25°F to 50°F and cutting the bake time almost in half. You can also refer to the chart opposite to determine the best cooking time for foods.

A Note About Salt

You may be surprised to learn that different brands and different types of salt can vary widely. For consistency in my recipes—both for flavor and for the nutrition information—I use Diamond Crystal Kosher. If you use another kind, just remember to taste as you go.

BASIC COOK TIMES

Follow the prep, temperature, and cook times below, and always remember to flip the foods halfway through cooking (or shake the basket for items like wings or fries).

		PREP	AIR FRYER TEMPERATURE	COOK TIME
MEAT & SEAFOOD	Bacon	center cut strips in a single layer	330°F	10 to 12 minutes
	Beef burger	½ inch thick	400°F	10 minutes for medium
	Calamari	½-inch-thick rings	400°F	3 to 5 minutes
	Chicken breast (boneless)	breaded thinly sliced chicken cutlet	400°F	7 to 8 minutes
	Chicken drumsticks	small, turning halfway	350°F	28 to 30 minutes
	Chicken thigh (boneless)	turning halfway	400°F	14 minutes
	Chicken wings (drumettes and wingettes)		400°F	22 to 24 minutes
	Cornish hen	halved	380°F	30 minutes
	Fish fillet (white fish, such as cod or halibut)	¾ to 1 inch thick	370°F	7 to 10 minutes
	Meatballs	¼ cup in size	380°F	9 to 10 minutes
	Pork chop (boneless)	¾ inch thick	400°F	8 minutes
	Roast beef	2 pounds	325°F	30 to 35 minutes for medium rare
	Salmon burger	¾ inch thick	400°F	12 minutes
	Salmon fillet	1 inch thick	400°F	7 minutes
	Sausage links	3 ounces each	400°F	10 to 12 minutes
	Shrimp (Jumbo size)	breaded	360°F	6 to 8 minutes
	Steak (sirloin, rib eye)	1 inch thick	400°F	10 minutes
VEGETABLES	Acorn squash	cut in half lengthwise and seeded	325°F	15 minutes
	Asparagus	ends trimmed, left whole or halved	370°F	8 to 10 minutes
	Baby red potatoes	quartered and tossed with oil	350°F	20 to 22 minutes
	Baked potato	7 ounces, whole	400°F	35 minutes
	Bell peppers	stemmed and seeded, cut into 1-inch-wide strips	350°F	10 minutes
	Broccoli	1-inch florets, tossed with oil	370°F	8 minutes
	Brussels sprouts	trimmed and halved if small, or quartered if large	350°F	10 to 13 minutes
	Cauliflower	small florets	380°F	8 minutes
	Eggplant	sliced ¼ inch thick	380°F	8 minutes
	French fries	¼-inch-thick batons	380°F	12 minutes
	Green beans	trimmed	370°F	8 to 9 minutes
	Mushrooms	halved, or quartered if large, and tossed with olive oil	370°F	8 to 10 minutes
	Onions	breaded and cut into rings	340°F	10 minutes
	Tomatoes	grape or cherry tomatoes, halved	400°F	10 minutes
	Zucchini or summer squash	halved and cut ½ inch thick	350°F	7 to 8 minutes

BREAKFAST

Q
V
GF
K
FF

Veggie-Leek and Cheese Frittata

Air fryers aren't just for french fries and chicken wings—baking dishes and cake pans expand the versatility of this appliance, allowing you to cook everything from eggs to cakes! To widen your air fryer capabilities, just purchase a set of inserts or use small baking dishes. This easy breakfast frittata is loaded with veggies, and it's as simple as mixing everything in a bowl, pouring it into a baking dish, then pressing start! Simple enough to make for breakfast or a weeknight dinner for two, frittatas are the way to go when you need a healthy dish to whip up fast.

Cooking spray

4 large eggs

4 ounces baby bella mushrooms, chopped

1 cup (1 ounce) baby spinach, chopped

1/3 cup (from 1 large) chopped leek, white part only

1/2 cup (2 ounces) shredded cheddar cheese

1/4 cup halved grape tomatoes

1 tablespoon 2% milk

1/2 teaspoon kosher salt

1/4 teaspoon garlic powder

1/4 teaspoon dried oregano

Freshly ground black pepper

Lightly spray a 6- or 7-inch round cake pan or baking dish with cooking spray.

In a large bowl, beat the eggs with a fork until uniform. Add the mushrooms, spinach, leek, cheddar, tomatoes, milk, salt, garlic powder, oregano, and pepper to taste. Mix to combine and pour into the baking dish.

Preheat the air fryer to 300°F.

Place the pan in the air fryer basket and cook for 20 to 23 minutes, until the eggs are set in the center. (For a toaster oven–style air fryer, cook in a small rectangular baking dish, about 5 1/2 x 7-inch, at 275°F for about 38 minutes.) Cut the frittata in half and serve.

skinny scoop The leek is the star of this frittata, but if you don't have any on hand, an onion will work. You can also swap the cheddar with Swiss cheese or Havarti.

PER SERVING: 1 piece • CALORIES 292 • FAT 19.5 g • SATURATED FAT 9 g • CHOLESTEROL 402 mg • CARBOHYDRATE 7 g • FIBER 1.5 g • PROTEIN 23 g • SUGARS 3 g • SODIUM 625 mg

Everything-but-the-Bagel Breakfast Pockets

What's your favorite breakfast sandwich? Turn it into a breakfast pocket! The filling combinations are endless: Bacon and cheese is usually my go-to, but you can swap the bacon for ham, or leave the meat out entirely and add more veggies. Whatever you do, don't leave off the "everything bagel" seasoning!

FILLING

4 slices center-cut bacon, chopped

1/3 cup diced red or green bell pepper

1/3 cup chopped scallions

4 large eggs

1/4 teaspoon kosher salt

Freshly ground black pepper

1/3 cup shredded cheddar cheese

DOUGH

1 cup (5 ounces) all-purpose flour, plus more for dusting

1 1/2 teaspoons baking powder

1/2 teaspoon kosher salt

1 cup 0% Greek yogurt (not regular yogurt), drained of any liquid

ASSEMBLY AND SERVING

1 large egg white, beaten

2 teaspoons "everything bagel" seasoning

Cooking spray

Hot sauce (optional)

For the filling: Place the bacon in a cold medium skillet. Turn the heat to medium and cook until browned and crispy, about 4 to 5 minutes. Use a slotted spoon to transfer to a plate lined with paper towels. Drain all but 1/2 tablespoon bacon fat from the pan. Add the bell pepper and scallions and cook, stirring occasionally, until soft, about 2 minutes.

Meanwhile, in a small bowl, beat the eggs with the salt and the pepper to taste. Add to the pan with the veggies and cook, stirring to scramble the eggs, until set, 2 to 3 minutes. Stir in the cheddar and remove from the heat. Set aside to cool while you make the dough.

For the dough: In a medium bowl, combine the flour, baking powder, and salt and whisk well. Add the yogurt and mix with a fork or spatula until well combined (it will look like small crumbles).

Lightly dust a work surface with flour. Transfer the dough to the work surface and knead for 2 to 3 minutes by hand until it is smooth and slightly tacky (it should not leave dough on your hand).

Divide the dough into 4 equal balls. Sprinkle the work surface and a rolling pin with flour. Roll each ball into a 7-inch round.

To assemble: Divide the cooked egg-veggie-cheese mixture (about 1/2 cup each) among the dough rounds, evenly spreading the filling over the bottom half of each and leaving a 1-inch border. Sprinkle each with one-quarter of the cooked bacon.

Brush the edges of the dough with the egg white and fold the top of the dough over the filling to make a half moon, leaving a 1/2-inch border uncovered at the bottom. Seal the edges by

PER SERVING: 1 pocket • CALORIES 305 • FAT 10.5 g • SATURATED FAT 4.5 g • CHOLESTEROL 203 mg • CARBOHYDRATE 28 g • FIBER 1.5 g • PROTEIN 21 g • SUGARS 3 g • SODIUM 839 mg

pinching the layers together or crimping with a fork. Poke the top 4 or 5 times with a fork, then brush with the egg white. Sprinkle each with ½ teaspoon of the "everything bagel" seasoning.

Preheat the air fryer to 350°F.

Spray the bottom of the air fryer basket with cooking spray to prevent sticking. Working in batches, arrange a single layer of the pockets in the air fryer basket. Bake for 6 minutes, then flip. Continue cooking another 4 minutes, or until golden. (For a toaster oven–style air fryer, bake at 300°F; the timing remains the same.) Serve with hot sauce, if desired.

skinny scoop Make sure the yogurt is Greek (not regular) and thick. I've tested this recipe with Fage and Stonyfield brands and they worked perfectly.

V
GF
DF
FF

PB&J Oatmeal Bake with Bananas and Blueberries

Peanut butter and jelly, a favorite childhood combination, is delicious when combined with warm baked oatmeal. Sweetened with overripe bananas and a touch of honey, then topped with some grape preserves, this dish almost feels like you're having dessert for breakfast! Since it's made in the air fryer, which is essentially a supercharged oven, it takes half the time to bake compared with a regular oven. Leftovers can be refrigerated and will taste just as good reheated for breakfast on the go.

Cooking spray

2 large very ripe bananas (the riper the better)

⅔ cup quick-cooking oats* (uncooked)

½ teaspoon baking powder

Pinch of kosher salt

½ cup unsweetened almond milk (or any milk you desire)

5 tablespoons peanut butter powder (such as PB2)

1 tablespoon honey

1 large egg

1 teaspoon vanilla extract

½ cup blueberries

4 tablespoons grape preserves (I like Polaner All Fruit Concord Grape Spreadable Fruit)

*Read the label to be sure this product is gluten-free.

Generously spray a 7-inch round cake pan with cooking spray.

In a medium bowl, mash the bananas well with a fork. In another medium bowl, stir together the oats, baking powder, and salt.

In a large bowl, whisk together the milk, peanut butter powder, honey, egg, and vanilla. Mix in the bananas until well incorporated, then add the oat mixture and combine. Fold in the blueberries. Pour into the prepared baking dish and spoon the jelly over the top by the teaspoon.

Preheat the air fryer to 300°F.

Place the baking dish in the air fryer basket. Bake for 25 minutes, or until the top is golden brown and the oatmeal is set in the center. (For a toaster oven–style air fryer, place the basket in the lower rack position and bake in a small rectangular baking dish at 250°F for about 36 minutes.) Remove and set aside to cool for 10 to 15 minutes. Slice into 4 wedges and serve warm.

PER SERVING: 1 wedge · CALORIES 226 · FAT 3.5 g · SATURATED FAT 0.5 g · CHOLESTEROL 47 mg · CARBOHYDRATE 44 g · FIBER 5 g · PROTEIN 7 g · SUGARS 23 g · SODIUM 183 mg

V
GF
DF

Home Fries with Onions and Peppers

Home fries will always remind me of my mom cooking behind the counter at her luncheonette when I was a teen. I waitressed at the luncheonette on weekends, and also had the job of peeling the potatoes for the home fries. This version is easier—no need to parboil or peel the potatoes, just make sure you dice them all the same size so they cook evenly. I love my home fries topped with two soft poached eggs and sometimes a few slices of bacon.

1 pound red potatoes, cut into ½-inch dice

1 medium onion, cut into ½-inch dice

1 large green bell pepper, cut into ½-inch dice

1 large red bell pepper, cut into ½-inch dice

1½ tablespoons extra-virgin olive oil

1¼ teaspoons kosher salt

¾ teaspoon garlic powder

¾ teaspoon sweet paprika

Freshly ground black pepper

In a large bowl, combine the potatoes, onion, bell peppers, oil, salt, garlic powder, paprika, and pepper to taste and toss well.

Preheat the air fryer to 350°F.

Add to the air fryer basket in one batch. Cook for about 35 minutes, shaking the basket every 10 minutes, until the potatoes are golden brown and soft in the center. (For a toaster oven–style air fryer, cook at 300°F for about 45 minutes.) Serve immediately.

PER SERVING: ⅔ cup • CALORIES 159 • FAT 5.5 g • SATURATED FAT 1 g • CHOLESTEROL 0 mg • CARBOHYDRATE 26 g • FIBER 4 g • PROTEIN 3 g • SUGARS 5 g • SODIUM 375 mg

SERVES
4

Q
V
GF

Homemade Bagels

My family is totally obsessed with these bagels! They're so easy to make totally from scratch and with just five (5!) ingredients: flour, Greek yogurt, egg whites, baking powder, and salt! No yeast, no boiling, no fancy mixer required. The addition of yogurt makes the bagels high in protein and taste so good that you may never buy bagels again. One must: Be sure your Greek yogurt is thick, or else your dough will be sticky. I've had best results with Stonyfield and Fage Greek yogurt (Chobani yields a sticky dough).

1 cup (5 ounces) unbleached all-purpose or whole wheat flour, plus more for dusting (see Skinny Scoop for gluten-free option)

2 teaspoons baking powder

¾ teaspoon kosher salt

1 cup 0% Greek yogurt (not regular yogurt), drained of any liquid

1 egg white, beaten

Optional toppings: "everything bagel" seasoning (sesame seeds, poppy seeds, dried garlic flakes, and dried onion flakes) or any of your favorite bagel toppings

In a medium bowl, combine the flour, baking powder, and salt and whisk well. Add the yogurt and mix with a fork or spatula until well combined (it will look like small crumbles).

Lightly dust a work surface with flour. Transfer the dough to the work surface and knead for 2 to 3 minutes by hand until it is smooth and slightly tacky (it should not leave dough on your hand when you pull it away). Divide the dough into 4 equal balls. Roll each ball into a ¾-inch-thick rope and join the ends to form bagels. Brush the tops with the egg white and sprinkle both sides with a topping of your choice, if desired.

Preheat the air fryer to 280°F.

Working in batches, place the bagels in the air fryer basket in a single layer. Bake for 15 to 16 minutes (no need to flip), until golden. (For a toaster oven–style air fryer, bake at 250°F for about 18 minutes.) Let cool for at least 15 minutes before cutting and serving.

skinny scoop
· Make sure your baking powder is not expired or your bagels won't rise.
· To make them gluten-free, try Cup4Cup gluten-free flour mix. Cook at 325°F for 12 minutes, flipping halfway through.

PER SERVING: 1 bagel · CALORIES 149 · FAT 0.5 g · SATURATED FAT 0 g · CHOLESTEROL 0 mg · CARBOHYDRATE 26 g · FIBER 1 g · PROTEIN 10 g · SUGARS 2 g · SODIUM 490 mg

V

Cinnamon Rolls with Cream Cheese Icing

A big mug of coffee with a hot cinnamon roll drizzled with a cream cheese topping makes for a wonderful, relaxing Sunday morning. Yes, you *can* eat cinnamon rolls: My philosophy is everything in moderation—nothing is off limits! These slimmed-down rolls use far less butter (just 2 teaspoons) and sugar than the traditional version, yet they still come out of the air fryer fluffy, delicious, and finger-licking good.

DOUGH

1⅛ teaspoons active dry yeast (about ½ envelope)

¼ cup warm water

2 teaspoons granulated sugar

2 tablespoons unsweetened almond milk or 2% milk

1 large egg

¼ teaspoon kosher salt

1½ cups (7½ ounces) all-purpose flour, sifted, plus more for dusting

2 teaspoons unsalted butter, melted

Cooking spray

FILLING

3 tablespoons light brown sugar

1½ teaspoons ground cinnamon

For the dough: In a small bowl, dissolve the yeast in the warm water and set aside for 5 minutes.

In a medium bowl, combine the granulated sugar, milk, egg, salt, yeast mixture, and 1 cup of the flour and whisk until smooth. Stir in the remaining ½ cup flour and use a wooden spoon to mix. When it gets too tough to mix with the spoon, use your hands to gently knead until it comes together in a ball (the dough will be a little sticky).

Turn the dough out onto a lightly floured surface and knead until the dough is completely smooth and elastic, about 8 minutes. Grease a large clean bowl with ½ teaspoon of the melted butter. Place the dough ball in the bowl, turning once to grease all over. Cover with a damp kitchen towel. Let the dough rise in a warm place until doubled in size, about 1 hour.

Coat a 7-inch round cake pan or pizza dish with cooking spray and set aside.

For the filling: In a small bowl, combine the brown sugar and cinnamon.

Punch down the dough. On a lightly floured surface, use a rolling pin to roll into a 7 x 13-inch rectangle, ¼ inch thick. Brush with the remaining 1½ teaspoons melted butter and sprinkle with the filling mixture. Cut into 7 strips 1 inch wide (a pizza cutter works great). Roll up each strip tightly. Place in

(recipe continues)

PER SERVING: **1 roll** · CALORIES **183** · FAT **3.5 g** · SATURATED FAT **2 g** · CHOLESTEROL **34 mg** · CARBOHYDRATE **33 g** · FIBER **1 g** · PROTEIN **5 g** · SUGARS **11 g** · SODIUM **92 mg**

GLAZE

¼ cup ⅓-less-fat cream cheese, at room temperature

¼ teaspoon vanilla extract

Pinch of kosher salt

¼ cup confectioners' sugar, sifted

Unsweetened almond milk, as needed

the prepared pan, spiral side up. Cover with a damp kitchen towel and set aside until the rolls have increased in size, 20 to 40 minutes.

Preheat the air fryer to 270°F.

Place the pan in the air fryer basket. Bake for 20 to 22 minutes, until golden brown. (For a toaster oven–style air fryer, place the basket in the lowest rack position and bake at 250°F for 23 to 25 minutes.) Let cool in the pan for 5 minutes while you prepare the glaze.

For the glaze: In a small bowl, whisk together the cream cheese, vanilla, and salt until completely smooth. Whisk in the confectioners' sugar until fully blended. Add the almond milk 1 teaspoon at a time, until the mixture reaches a pourable, but still thick, consistency.

Spread the glaze evenly over the warm cinnamon rolls in the pan, making sure the tops of the rolls are completely covered. Serve warm.

skinny scoop Refrigerate the leftovers, then pop them in the air fryer or microwave to reheat.

Q
GF
DF
K
FF

Breakfast Turkey Sausage

Sausage for breakfast is never a bad idea, but buying premade patties or links means lots of fat and processed ingredients. When you make them from scratch, you can control what goes in, and believe it or not, they are simple to make! These breakfast sausage patties use ground turkey to keep them lean and are naturally sweetened with minced apple.

1 tablespoon chopped fresh sage

1 tablespoon chopped fresh thyme

1¼ teaspoons kosher salt

1 teaspoon fennel seeds, crushed with the side of a knife

¾ teaspoon smoked paprika

½ teaspoon garlic powder

½ teaspoon onion powder

⅛ teaspoon freshly ground black pepper

⅛ teaspoon crushed red pepper flakes

1 pound 93% lean ground turkey

½ cup finely minced sweet apple (peeled), such as Gala or Honeycrisp

In a medium bowl, combine the sage, thyme, salt, fennel seeds, paprika, garlic powder, onion powder, black pepper, and pepper flakes and mix well. Add the turkey and apple and work the spice mixture into the meat with your hands until well blended. Shape into 8 patties, about ¼ inch thick and 3 inches in diameter.

Preheat the air fryer to 400°F.

Working in batches, arrange a single layer of the patties in the air fryer basket. Cook for 10 minutes, flipping halfway, until the meat is browned and cooked through in the center. (For a toaster oven–style air fryer, the temperature and timing remain the same.) Serve warm.

skinny scoop These patties can be made a day ahead or can be frozen, uncooked, for up to 1 month.

PER SERVING: **2 patties** · CALORIES **185** · FAT **9.5 g** · SATURATED FAT **2.5 g** · CHOLESTEROL **84 mg** · CARBOHYDRATE **3 g** · FIBER **1 g** · PROTEIN **22 g** · SUGARS **2 g** · SODIUM **430 mg**

Petite Spiced Pumpkin Bread

Pumpkin bread may be a fall favorite, but since it's made with a lot of butter, it's not necessarily a winner for people watching their weight. I whipped up a lighter version so you can enjoy it all season long. I use a combination of unbleached and white whole wheat flour, which has a more neutral flavor than regular whole wheat.

Cooking spray

1/3 cup unbleached all-purpose or gluten-free flour (see Skinny Scoop)

1/4 cup white whole wheat or gluten-free flour

5 tablespoons loosely packed light brown sugar

1/4 teaspoon baking soda

1/4 teaspoon baking powder

1 teaspoon pumpkin pie spice

1/8 teaspoon ground cinnamon

1/8 teaspoon ground nutmeg

1/8 teaspoon kosher salt

3/4 cup canned unsweetened pumpkin puree

1 tablespoon coconut or vegetable oil

1 large egg

3/4 teaspoon vanilla extract

CRUMB TOPPING

2 tablespoons light brown sugar

1/2 tablespoon white whole wheat or gluten-free flour

1/8 teaspoon ground cinnamon

1/2 tablespoon cold unsalted butter

Spray a 6 × 3½ × 2-inch mini loaf pan with cooking spray.

In a medium bowl, whisk together the flours, brown sugar, baking soda, baking powder, pumpkin pie spice, cinnamon, nutmeg, and salt.

In a large bowl, combine the pumpkin puree, oil, egg, and vanilla. Beat with an electric hand mixer on medium speed, pausing to scrape down the sides of the bowl with a spatula, until thick.

Add the flour mixture to the pumpkin mixture and mix on low speed until combined. Pour the batter into the prepared pan.

For the crumb topping: In a small bowl, combine the brown sugar, flour, and cinnamon. Cut the butter in with a fork until the mixture resembles coarse crumbs. Evenly sprinkle over the batter.

Preheat the air fryer to 300°F.

Place the pan in the air fryer basket. Bake for 40 to 45 minutes, until a toothpick inserted in the center comes out clean. (For a toaster oven–style air fryer, place the basket in the lower rack position and bake at 250°F for about 45 minutes.) Let cool for at least 30 minutes before cutting into 6 slices to serve.

skinny scoop
- You can find mini foil loaf pans in the foil pan section of most supermarkets.
- To make it gluten-free, swap the flours for a good gluten-free flour mix such as Cup4Cup.

PER SERVING: 1 slice · CALORIES 139 · FAT 4.5 g · SATURATED FAT 3 g · CHOLESTEROL 34 mg · CARBOHYDRATE 23 g · FIBER 2 g · PROTEIN 3 g · SUGARS 11 g · SODIUM 113 mg

Q
V
GF

Blueberry-Lemon Yogurt Muffins

There's nothing quite like a delicious blueberry muffin for breakfast. These are fluffy, lightly sweetened, and loaded with blueberries, and (bonus!) you don't even need to use a muffin pan. I pour the batter into lined foil baking cups and put them right in the air fryer basket. Six muffins are the perfect amount to keep you from getting into too much trouble. If you can't find fresh berries, frozen work just as well (no need to thaw).

Cooking spray

1½ tablespoons unsalted butter, at room temperature

6 tablespoons sugar

1 large egg

1 large egg white

1 teaspoon vanilla extract

1 teaspoon fresh lemon juice

Grated zest of 1 lemon

5 ounces (10 tablespoons) 0% Greek yogurt

¾ cup plus 2 tablespoons self-rising cake flour (I like Presto; see Skinny Scoop for gluten-free option)

¾ cup fresh or frozen blueberries

Spray 6 lined foil baking cups with cooking spray.

In a medium bowl, with an electric hand mixer, beat the butter and sugar on medium speed until well combined, about 2 minutes.

In a small bowl, whisk together the whole egg, egg white, and vanilla. Add to the butter and sugar mixture along with the lemon juice and zest and beat until combined, about 30 seconds. Beat in the yogurt, then the flour, mixing on low speed until combined, about 30 seconds. Using a spatula, fold in the blueberries. Using an ice cream scoop, evenly divide the mixture among the prepared baking cups, filling them three-quarters of the way full.

Preheat the air fryer to 300°F.

Working in batches, place the muffins in the air fryer basket. Bake for 15 minutes, or until the tops are golden and a toothpick inserted in the center comes out clean. (For a toaster oven–style air fryer, the temperature remains the same; bake for about 14 minutes.) Let cool before eating.

skinny scoop To make them gluten-free, replace the self-rising flour with ¾ cup gluten-free flour mix, such as Cup4Cup, and add ¼ teaspoon baking soda.

PER SERVING: 1 muffin · CALORIES 168 · FAT 3.5 g · SATURATED FAT 2 g · CHOLESTEROL 40 mg · CARBOHYDRATE 28 g · FIBER 0.5 g · PROTEIN 5 g · SUGARS 16 g · SODIUM 225 mg

APPETIZERS & SNACKS

Buffalo Wings with Blue Cheese Dip

Be prepared to get your fingers messy! Not only are these Buffalo wings flavorful, but they'll also save you a ton of calories (thanks to the air fryer) compared with your average deep-fried, greasy, restaurant version. The simple, cooling blue cheese dip is made with Greek yogurt and is also perfect for dipping celery and carrot sticks.

12 pieces (26 ounces) chicken wing portions (a mix of drumettes and wingettes)

6 tablespoons Frank's RedHot sauce

2 tablespoons distilled white vinegar

1 teaspoon dried oregano

1 teaspoon garlic powder

½ teaspoon kosher salt

BLUE CHEESE DIP

¼ cup crumbled blue cheese

⅓ cup 2% Greek yogurt

½ tablespoon fresh lemon juice

½ tablespoon distilled white vinegar

2 celery stalks, halved crosswise and cut into 8 sticks total

2 medium carrots, peeled, halved crosswise and cut into 8 sticks total

In a large bowl, combine the chicken with 1 tablespoon of the hot sauce, the vinegar, oregano, garlic powder, and salt, tossing to coat well.

For the blue cheese dip: In a small bowl, mash the blue cheese and yogurt together with a fork. Stir in the lemon juice and vinegar until well blended. Refrigerate until ready to serve.

Preheat the air fryer to 400°F.

Working in batches, arrange a single layer of the chicken in the air fryer basket. Cook for 22 minutes, flipping halfway, until crispy, browned, and cooked through. (For a toaster oven–style air fryer, the temperature remains the same; cook for 15 to 16 minutes.) Transfer to a large clean bowl (do not use the bowl the marinade was in). When all the batches are done, return all the chicken to the air fryer and cook for 1 minute to heat through.

Return the chicken to the bowl and toss with the remaining 5 tablespoons hot sauce to coat. Arrange on a platter and serve with the celery, carrot sticks, and blue cheese dip.

skinny scoop To prep the wings ahead of time, you can marinate the chicken and make the dip the night before.

PER SERVING: **3 pieces chicken + 2 carrot sticks + 2 celery sticks + 2 tablespoons dip** • CALORIES **256** • FAT **16.5 g** • SATURATED FAT **6 g** • CHOLESTEROL **226 mg** • CARBOHYDRATE **5 g** • FIBER **1.5 g** • PROTEIN **23 g** • SUGARS **3 g** • SODIUM **1,120 mg**

Chicken-Vegetable Spring Rolls

I love spring rolls so much I can literally eat them cold right out of the refrigerator (am I the only one?). There are so many things to love about making spring rolls from scratch: Air-frying them means less mess and very little oil, so they're healthier. Plus, they're so easy to assemble. Let's just say they're perfection in every bite!

1 tablespoon toasted sesame oil

½ pound 93% lean ground chicken (see Skinny Scoop for vegetarian option)

4 tablespoons reduced-sodium soy sauce

1 teaspoon grated fresh ginger

3 garlic cloves, minced

2 large scallions, chopped

2 cups shredded napa or green cabbage

1 cup chopped baby bok choy

½ cup shredded carrots

1 tablespoon unseasoned rice vinegar

10 spring roll wrappers (8-inch square; made with wheat, not rice)

Olive oil spray

Thai sweet chili sauce, duck sauce, or hot sauce, for dipping (optional)

In a large skillet, heat the sesame oil over high heat. Add the chicken and 2 tablespoons of the soy sauce and cook, breaking it up with a wooden spoon, until the chicken is just cooked through, about 5 minutes. Add the ginger, garlic, and scallions. Cook, stirring, until fragrant, about 30 seconds. Add the cabbage, bok choy, carrots, the remaining 2 tablespoons soy sauce, and the vinegar. Cook, stirring occasionally, until the vegetables are crisp-tender, 2 to 3 minutes. Set aside to cool.

Working with one at a time, place a wrapper on a clean surface, the points facing top and bottom like a diamond. Spoon ¼ cup of the mixture onto the bottom third of the wrapper. Dip your finger in a small bowl of water and run it along the edges of the wrapper. Lift the point nearest you and wrap it around the filling. Fold the left and right corners in toward the center and continue to roll into a tight cylinder. Set aside and repeat with the remaining wrappers and filling.

Preheat the air fryer to 400°F.

Spray all sides of the rolls with oil. Working in batches, arrange a single layer of the rolls in the air fryer basket. Cook for 6 to 8 minutes, flipping halfway, until browned. (For a toaster oven–style air fryer, cook at 325°F for 6 to 7 minutes.) Serve with dipping sauce on the side, if desired.

skinny scoop

· For variations, you can swap out the chicken for ground pork or minced shrimp, or use chopped portobello mushrooms to make them vegetarian.

· If you can't find spring roll wrappers, egg roll wrappers (such as Nasoya brand) will work, too.

PER SERVING: **2 rolls** · CALORIES **166** · FAT **6.5 g** · SATURATED FAT **1.5 g** · CHOLESTEROL **39 mg** · CARBOHYDRATE **16 g** · FIBER **1.5 g** · PROTEIN **10 g** · SUGARS **2 g** · SODIUM **538 mg**

Q
GF
K

Bacon-Wrapped Cheesy Jalapeño Poppers

These heavenly cheese-stuffed, bacon-wrapped jalapeños are a winner when I need a quick and easy snack or game-day appetizer. You can make as many or as few as you wish, and they can be prepped ahead of time, so just pop them in the air fryer when friends arrive. The bacon crisps up beautifully in the air fryer, and bonus, you don't have to heat the whole oven to whip them up.

6 large jalapeños

4 ounces ⅓-less-fat cream cheese

¼ cup (1 ounce) shredded reduced-fat sharp cheddar cheese*

2 scallions, green tops only, sliced

6 slices center-cut bacon, halved

*Read the label to be sure this product is gluten-free.

Wearing rubber gloves, halve the jalapeños lengthwise to make 12 pieces. Scoop out the seeds and membranes and discard.

In a medium bowl, combine the cream cheese, cheddar, and scallions. Using a small spoon or spatula, fill the jalapeños with the cream cheese filling. Wrap a bacon strip around each pepper and secure with a toothpick.

Preheat the air fryer to 325°F.

Working in batches, place the stuffed peppers in a single layer in the air fryer basket. Cook for about 12 minutes, until the peppers are tender, the bacon is browned and crisp, and the cheese is melted. (For a toaster oven–style air fryer, cook at 300°F; the timing remains the same.) Serve warm.

PER SERVING: **2 pieces** · CALORIES **95** · FAT **6.5 g** · SATURATED FAT **3.5 g** · CHOLESTEROL **17 mg** · CARBOHYDRATE **3 g** · FIBER **0.5 g** · PROTEIN **6 g** · SUGARS **1 g** · SODIUM **208 mg**

Q

Crab and Cream Cheese Wontons

You get it all with these crab rangoons! Often found in American Chinese and Thai restaurants, these crispy pockets of sweet crab, cream cheese, and scallions will have your taste buds dancing. My recipe contains less cream cheese and more crab than the take-out version, and they get so crispy in the air fryer—you won't miss the grease at all!

4 ounces ⅓-less-fat cream cheese, at room temperature

2½ ounces (½ cup) lump crabmeat, picked over for bits of shell

2 scallions, chopped

2 garlic cloves, finely minced

2 teaspoons reduced-sodium soy sauce

15 wonton wrappers

1 large egg white, beaten

5 tablespoons Thai sweet chili sauce, for dipping

In a medium bowl, combine the cream cheese, crab, scallions, garlic, and soy sauce. Mix with a fork until thoroughly combined.

Working with one at a time, place a wonton wrapper on a clean surface, the points facing top and bottom like a diamond. Spoon 1 level tablespoon of the crab mixture onto the center of the wrapper. Dip your finger in a small bowl of water and run it along the edges of the wrapper. Take one corner of the wrapper and fold it up to the opposite corner, forming a triangle. Gently press out any air between wrapper and filling and seal the edges. Set aside and repeat with the remaining wrappers and filling. Brush both sides of the wontons with egg white.

Preheat the air fryer to 340°F.

Working in batches, arrange a single layer of the wontons in the air fryer basket. Cook for about 8 minutes, flipping halfway, until golden brown and crispy. (For a toaster oven-style air fryer, cook at 300°F; the timing remains the same.) Serve hot with the chili sauce for dipping.

PER SERVING: **3 wontons + 1 tablespoon sauce** · CALORIES **180** · FAT **4.5 g** · SATURATED FAT **2.5 g** · CHOLESTEROL **29 mg** · CARBOHYDRATE **26 g** · FIBER **0.5 g** · PROTEIN **9 g** · SUGARS **7 g** · SODIUM **577 mg**

Baked Clam Dip

If you love baked clams, you'll love this hot, creamy dip made with all of the same savory flavors, but with much less work! Making this in the air fryer is perfect for small gatherings—it's always a crowd-pleaser and you don't have to heat your whole oven. I like to serve the dip with raw veggies, but whole-grain crackers or baked chips are great, too.

Cooking spray

2 (6.5-ounce) cans chopped clams, in clam juice

⅓ cup panko bread crumbs, regular or gluten-free

1 medium garlic clove, minced

1 tablespoon olive oil

1 tablespoon fresh lemon juice

¼ teaspoon Tabasco sauce

½ teaspoon onion powder

¼ teaspoon dried oregano

¼ teaspoon freshly ground black pepper

⅛ teaspoon kosher salt

½ teaspoon sweet paprika

2½ tablespoons freshly grated Parmesan cheese

2 celery stalks, cut into 2-inch pieces

Spray a 5½- to 6½-inch round baking dish with cooking spray.

Drain one of the cans of clams. Place in a medium bowl along with the remaining can of clams (including the juice), the panko, garlic, olive oil, lemon juice, Tabasco sauce, onion powder, oregano, pepper, salt, ¼ teaspoon of the paprika, and 2 tablespoons of the Parmesan. Mix well and let sit for 10 minutes. Transfer to the baking dish.

Preheat the air fryer to 325°F.

Place the baking dish in the air fryer basket and cook for 10 minutes. Top with the remaining ¼ teaspoon paprika and ½ tablespoon Parmesan. Cook for about 8 more minutes, until golden brown on top. (For a toaster oven–style air fryer, the temperature remains the same; cook for 10 minutes, then 2 to 3 more minutes.) Serve hot, with the celery for dipping.

PER SERVING: ¼ cup dip + 4 celery sticks · CALORIES 104 · FAT 3.5 g · SATURATED FAT 1 g · CHOLESTEROL 28 mg · CARBOHYDRATE 6 g · FIBER 0.5 g · PROTEIN 11 g · SUGARS 0.5 g · SODIUM 118 mg

Cheesy Crab-Stuffed Mushrooms

Crab and cheese—what's *not* to love about this combo? I add the perfect pair to my famous stuffed mushrooms to create an unbelievably delicious appetizer. Serve as a side dish to steak for a fun spin on surf and turf.

16 large white mushrooms

Olive oil spray

¼ teaspoon kosher salt

6 ounces (1 cup) lump crabmeat, picked over for bits of shell

⅓ cup freshly grated Parmesan cheese

¼ cup panko bread crumbs, regular or gluten-free

3 tablespoons mayonnaise

2 tablespoons chopped scallions

1 large egg, beaten

1 garlic clove, minced

¾ teaspoon Old Bay seasoning

1 tablespoon chopped fresh parsley

½ cup (2 ounces) shredded mozzarella cheese

Wipe the mushrooms with a damp paper towel to clean. Remove the stems, finely chop, and set aside. Spray the mushroom caps with oil and sprinkle with the salt.

In a medium bowl, combine the crab, Parmesan, panko, mayonnaise, chopped mushroom stems, scallions, egg, garlic, Old Bay, and parsley. Mound the filling (about 2 tablespoons each) onto each mushroom cap. Top each with ½ tablespoon mozzarella, pressing to stick to the crab.

Preheat the air fryer to 360°F.

Working in batches, arrange a single layer of the stuffed mushrooms in the air fryer basket. Cook for 8 to 10 minutes, until the mushrooms are soft, the crab is hot, and the cheese is golden. (For a toaster oven–style air fryer, cook at 300°F for about 10 minutes.) Serve hot.

skinny scoop This can be prepared ahead of time, refrigerated, and cooked just before serving.

PER SERVING: **2 stuffed mushrooms** · CALORIES **125** · FAT **8 g** · SATURATED FAT **2.5 g** · CHOLESTEROL **55 mg** · CARBOHYDRATE **4 g** · FIBER **0.5 g** · PROTEIN **10 g** · SUGARS **1 g** · SODIUM **375 mg**

Ahi Poke Wonton Cups

Making wonton cups in the air fryer requires a little creativity, but with some cupcake liners and dried beans to weight them down, they come out perfectly crisp. They're the ideal vessels to serve this delicious poke salad made with tuna, avocado, and cucumber. So good, in fact, that you may want to double the recipe!

12 wonton wrappers

Olive oil spray

¾ cup dried beans (for weighting the cups)

2 tablespoons reduced-sodium soy sauce

1 teaspoon toasted sesame oil

½ teaspoon Sriracha sauce

¼ pound fresh sushi-grade ahi tuna, cut into ½-inch cubes

¼ cup peeled, seeded, and diced cucumber

2 ounces Hass avocado (about ½ small), cut into ½-inch cubes

¼ cup sliced scallions

1½ teaspoons toasted sesame seeds

Place each wonton wrapper in a lined foil baking cup, pressing gently in the middle and against the sides to create a bowl. Spray each lightly with oil. Add 1 heaping tablespoon of dried beans to the middle of each cup (this helps weight down the wrapper and keep the wontons in place during cooking).

Preheat the air fryer to 280°F.

Working in batches, arrange a single layer of the cups in the air fryer basket. Cook for 8 to 10 minutes, until browned and crispy. (For a toaster oven–style air fryer, cook at 250°F; the timing remains the same.) Carefully remove the cups and let cool slightly. Remove the beans and set the cups aside.

Meanwhile, in a medium bowl, combine the soy sauce, sesame oil, and Sriracha. Whisk well to combine. Add the tuna, cucumber, avocado, and scallions and toss gently to combine.

Add 2 heaping tablespoons of the ahi mixture to each cup and top each with ⅛ teaspoon sesame seeds. Serve immediately.

PER SERVING: **3 poke wonton cups** · CALORIES **147** · FAT **4.5 g** · SATURATED FAT **0.5 g** · CHOLESTEROL **15 mg** · CARBOHYDRATE **17 g** · FIBER **2 g** · PROTEIN **10 g** · SUGARS **0.5 g** · SODIUM **427 mg**

Q
V
GF
DF

Homemade Chips and Salsa

It's so easy to make your own restaurant-quality chips and salsa! These chips come out crisp after mere minutes in the air fryer. They're perfect for snacking or dipping (also great with guacamole!) and so much better than the chips you'd buy at the store. We love them sprinkled with chile-lime seasoning salt (such as Tajín brand), which gives them a lime-y tang, but a few pinches of salt would be fine, too.

SALSA

¼ small onion

2 small garlic cloves

½ jalapeño, seeds and membranes removed (or leave in if you like it spicy)

1 (14.5-ounce) can diced tomatoes, undrained (not with basil; I like Tuttorosso)

Handful of fresh cilantro

Juice of 1 lime

¼ teaspoon kosher salt

CHIPS

6 corn tortillas

Olive oil spray

¾ teaspoon chile-lime seasoning salt (such as Tajín or Trader Joe's)

For the salsa: In a food processor, combine the onion, garlic, jalapeño, tomatoes (including the juices), cilantro, lime juice, and salt. Pulse a few times until combined and chunky (don't overprocess). Transfer to a serving bowl.

For the chips: Spray both sides of the tortillas with oil. Stack the tortillas on top of each other so they line up. Using a large sharp knife, cut them in half, then in quarters, and once more so they are divided into 8 equal wedges each (48 total). Spread out on a work surface and season both sides with chile-lime salt.

Preheat the air fryer to 400°F.

Working in batches, arrange a single layer of the tortilla wedges in the air fryer basket. Cook for 5 to 6 minutes, shaking the basket halfway, until golden and crisp (be careful not to burn them). (For a toaster oven–style air fryer, cook at 350°F for 4 to 5 minutes.) Let cool a few minutes before serving with the salsa.

PER SERVING 12 chips + ¾ cup salsa · CALORIES 121 · FAT 1 g · SATURATED FAT 0 g · CHOLESTEROL 0 mg · CARBOHYDRATE 25 g · FIBER 3.5 g · PROTEIN 2 g · SUGARS 4 g · SODIUM 698 mg

Tomatillo Salsa Verde

This is a great recipe for salsa verde that goes well with pretty much anything. It's so easy to make, plus no need to heat up a whole oven to do it. I love this salsa with chips (see page 46), but it's also delicious with chicken, burgers, scrambled eggs, roasted vegetables, steak, or simply eaten with a spoon standing at the fridge. In fact, I've yet to find something that it does *not* go well with. You'll never buy the jarred stuff again!

1 large poblano pepper

1 large jalapeño

¼ small onion

2 garlic cloves

Olive oil spray

¾ pound tomatillos (husks removed)

3 tablespoons chopped fresh cilantro

¼ teaspoon sugar (omit for keto diets)

1 teaspoon kosher salt

Preheat the air fryer to 400°F.

Spritz the poblano, jalapeño, onion, and garlic with olive oil, then transfer to the air fryer basket. Cook for about 14 minutes, flipping halfway, until charred on top. (For a toaster oven-style air fryer, the temperature remains the same; cook for 10 minutes.) Remove the poblano, wrap in foil, and let it cool for 10 minutes. Remove the remaining vegetables from the basket and transfer to a food processor.

Spritz the tomatillos with oil and place in the air fryer basket. Cook for 10 minutes, flipping halfway, until charred. (For a toaster oven-style air fryer, the temperature and timing remain the same.) Transfer to the food processor with the other vegetables.

Unwrap the foil from the poblano. Peel the skin off and remove the seeds. Transfer to the food processor along with the cilantro, sugar (if using), and salt. Pulse the mixture until the ingredients are coarsely chopped. Add 5 to 6 tablespoons water and pulse until a coarse puree forms. Transfer the salsa to a serving dish.

PER SERVING: ¼ cup • CALORIES 42 • FAT 1 g • SATURATED FAT 0 g • CHOLESTEROL 0 mg • CARBOHYDRATE 8 g • FIBER 2 g • PROTEIN 1 g • SUGARS 5 g • SODIUM 284 mg

Q
GF
DF

Devils on Horseback

Cooking rule #353: Wrap anything in bacon and it's bound to be good! This easy appetizer with a very odd name combines salty and sweet flavors with crispy and creamy textures. You can prepare the prunes ahead of time and pop them in the air fryer when your guests arrive for easy entertaining.

24 petite pitted prunes (4½ ounces)

¼ cup crumbled blue cheese (see Skinny Scoop for dairy-free option)

8 slices center-cut bacon, cut crosswise into thirds

Halve the prunes lengthwise, but don't cut them all the way through. Place ½ teaspoon of cheese in the center of each prune. Wrap a piece of bacon around each prune and secure the bacon with a toothpick.

Preheat the air fryer to 400°F.

Working in batches, arrange a single layer of the prunes in the air fryer basket. Cook for about 7 minutes, flipping halfway, until the bacon is cooked through and crisp. (For a toaster oven–style air fryer, temperature remains the same; cook for 6 minutes.) Let cool slightly and serve warm.

skinny scoop
- Pitted dates can be used in place of prunes.
- To make the dish dairy-free, swap the cheese for slivered almonds.

PER SERVING: **2 prunes** · CALORIES **55** · FAT **2.5 g** · SATURATED FAT **1 g** · CHOLESTEROL **4 mg** · CARBOHYDRATE **7 g** · FIBER **1 g** · PROTEIN **3 g** · SUGARS **4 g** · SODIUM **119 mg**

Loaded Zucchini Skins

You won't miss the carbs in these zucchini skins loaded with all the fixin's that you'd normally get on potato skins. Karina, my older daughter, who loves zucchini, declares them her new favorite food—even better than pizza, whoa! The stuffed zucchini make a great appetizer, side dish, or afternoon snack, plus, they're a great way to get your kids to eat veggies.

3 slices center-cut bacon

2 large zucchini (about 9 ounces each)

Olive oil spray

¾ teaspoon kosher salt

¼ teaspoon garlic powder

¼ teaspoon sweet paprika

Freshly ground black pepper

1¼ cups (5 ounces) shredded cheddar cheese

8 teaspoons light sour cream or 2% plain Greek yogurt

2 scallions, green tops only, sliced

Preheat the air fryer to 350°F.

Place the bacon in the air fryer basket. Cook for about 10 minutes, flipping halfway, until crisp. (For a toaster oven-style air fryer, the temperature remains the same; cook for about 8 minutes.) Place on paper towels to drain, then coarsely chop.

Halve the zucchini lengthwise, then crosswise (you'll have 8 pieces). Scoop the pulp out of each piece, leaving a ¼-inch shell on all sides (save the pulp for another use, such as adding to omelets or soup).

Place the zucchini skins on a work surface. Spray both sides with olive oil, then season all over with the salt. Season the cut side with the garlic powder, paprika, and pepper to taste.

Preheat the air fryer to 350°F again.

Working in batches, arrange a single layer of the zucchini in the air fryer basket. Cook for about 8 minutes, or until crisp-tender. Remove from the basket and place 2½ tablespoons cheddar inside each skin and top with the bacon.

Working in batches again, return the stuffed zucchini in a single layer to the air fryer basket. Cook until the cheese is melted, about 2 minutes. (For a toaster oven-style air fryer, the temperature and timing remain the same.) Top each with 1 teaspoon sour cream and the scallions and serve immediately.

PER SERVING: **2 skins** · CALORIES **101** · FAT **7.5 g** · SATURATED FAT **4.5 g** · CHOLESTEROL **21 mg** · CARBOHYDRATE **3 g** · FIBER **1 g** · PROTEIN **6 g** · SUGARS **2 g** · SODIUM **269 mg**

Q
GF

Cauliflower Rice Arancini

I love Italian rice balls, which are traditionally filled with rice, sausage, and cheese, then breaded and fried. My lighter version replaces the rice with cauliflower and instead of frying, they're tossed into the air fryer where they cook until perfectly golden (and with much less oil and calories). The trick to making them is adding the mozzarella cheese to the cauliflower mixture while the cauliflower is hot—the cheese acts like glue, holding everything together, so it's easier to roll into a ball.

2 (2.75-ounce) sweet Italian chicken sausage links,* casings removed

4½ cups riced cauliflower (frozen)

½ teaspoon kosher salt

1¼ cups marinara sauce

1 cup (4 ounces) shredded part-skim mozzarella cheese*

Cooking spray

2 large eggs

½ cup bread crumbs, regular or gluten-free

2 tablespoons freshly grated Pecorino Romano or Parmesan cheese

*Read the label to be sure this product is gluten-free.

Heat a large skillet over medium-high heat. Add the sausage and cook, breaking the meat up with a spoon as small as you can, until cooked through, 4 to 5 minutes.

Add the cauliflower, salt, and ¼ cup of the marinara. Reduce the heat to medium and cook, stirring occasionally, until the cauliflower is tender and heated through, 6 to 7 minutes. Remove from the heat and add the mozzarella to the skillet, stirring well to mix. Let it cool slightly until it's easy to handle with your hands but still hot, 3 to 4 minutes.

Spray a ¼-cup measuring cup with cooking spray and pack tightly with the cauliflower mixture, leveling the top. Use a small spoon to scoop it out into your palm and roll into a ball. Set aside on a dish. Repeat with the remaining cauliflower (you should have 12 balls).

In a small bowl, beat the eggs with 1 tablespoon water until smooth. In a second bowl, combine the bread crumbs and pecorino.

Working one at a time, dip a cauliflower ball in the egg, then in the crumbs, gently pressing to adhere. Transfer to a work surface and spray all over with oil. Repeat with the remaining cauliflower balls.

Preheat the air fryer to 400°F.

Working in batches, arrange a single layer of the cauliflower balls in the air fryer basket. Cook for about 9 minutes,

PER SERVING: **3 balls + ¼ cup marinara** · CALORIES **293** · FAT **13 g** · SATURATED FAT **5.5 g** · CHOLESTEROL **140 mg** · CARBOHYDRATE **21 g** · FIBER **4 g** · PROTEIN **23 g** · SUGARS **5 g** · SODIUM **887 mg**

flipping halfway, until the crumbs are golden and the center is hot. (For a toaster oven–style air fryer, cook at 350°F for 6 to 7 minutes.)

Meanwhile, warm up the remaining 1 cup marinara for serving.

Serve the arancini with the warm marinara for dipping.

Crispy Za'atar Chickpeas

Roasted chickpeas are a healthy—yet admittedly addictive—snack that is so quick and easy to make in the air fryer. They become nutty and crunchy once they're roasted. Here, I've tossed them with garlic powder and za'atar—a Middle Eastern blend of sumac, thyme, sesame, and salt—but you can use any spice combination you like, such as Indian-inspired flavors (cumin, curry powder, garlic powder, and salt) or just garlicky (garlic powder, salt, and pepper). Really, the possibilities are endless.

1 (15-ounce) can chickpeas, rinsed and drained*

⅛ teaspoon kosher salt

1 teaspoon za'atar spice blend

¼ teaspoon garlic powder

Extra-virgin olive oil spray

*Read the label to be sure this product is gluten-free.

Place the chickpeas on a plate lined with paper towels. Pat with paper towels and let stand to dry completely.

In a small bowl, combine the salt, za'atar, and garlic powder.

Preheat the air fryer to 375°F.

Place half of the chickpeas in the air fryer basket in a single layer. Cook, shaking the basket every 5 minutes, until crunchy all the way through (no longer moist) and golden brown on the outside, about 12 minutes. (For a toaster oven–style air fryer, cook at 350°F for 10 minutes.)

Transfer the chickpeas to a medium bowl. Lightly spray all over with olive oil and immediately toss with half of the spices while hot. When the second batch is cooked, spray with oil and toss with the remaining spices. Let cool and eat at room temperature.

skinny scoop You can make your own za'atar blend by combining 1 tablespoon each dried thyme, ground sumac, ground cumin, and toasted sesame seeds, plus 1 teaspoon kosher salt.

PER SERVING: ½ cup • CALORIES 118 • FAT 2 g • SATURATED FAT 0 g • CHOLESTEROL 0 mg • CARBOHYDRATE 20 g • FIBER 4 g • PROTEIN 6 g • SUGARS 0 g • SODIUM 226 mg

Q
V
GF

Garlic Knots

These soft, garlicky knots taste like they come straight from your favorite pizzeria but are made entirely from scratch using my easy yeast-free bagel dough recipe. No need for the dough to rise, no fancy mixer required, and no waiting for the delivery guy! Simply knead the dough by hand, roll, and air-fry. These are great with tomatoes: Tommy loves serving the knots with his summer tomato salad, and I like them with a hot bowl of tomato soup. For the most traditional route, serve as an appetizer with a side of marinara sauce for dipping.

1 cup (5 ounces) all-purpose or white whole wheat flour (see Skinny Scoop for gluten-free option), plus more for dusting

2 teaspoons baking powder

¾ teaspoon kosher salt

1 cup 0% Greek yogurt (not regular yogurt), drained of any liquid

Olive oil spray

2 teaspoons unsalted butter

3 garlic cloves, minced

1 tablespoon grated Parmesan cheese

1 tablespoon finely chopped fresh parsley

Warmed marinara sauce (optional), for serving

In a large bowl, whisk together the flour, baking powder, and salt. Add the yogurt and mix with a fork or spatula until well combined (it will look like small crumbles).

Lightly dust a work surface with flour. Transfer the dough to the work surface and knead for 2 to 3 minutes by hand until it is smooth and slightly tacky (it should not leave dough on your hand when you pull it away). Divide the dough into 8 balls. Roll each ball into ropes, about 9 inches long. Tie each rope into a "knot" ball. Place on the work surface and spray the tops with olive oil.

Preheat the air fryer to 250°F.

Working in batches, place a single layer of the knots in the air fryer basket. Bake for 22 to 24 minutes (no need to flip), until the tops are golden. (For a toaster oven–style air fryer, the temperature remains the same; bake for 18 to 20 minutes.) Remove from the basket and let cool for 5 minutes (they will continue cooking in the center).

Meanwhile, in a nonstick medium skillet, melt the butter over low heat. Add the garlic and cook, stirring frequently, until golden, about 2 minutes.

Toss the knots in the skillet with the melted butter and garlic (or use a brush to coat the knots with the garlic butter). If the knots are too dry, give them another spritz of olive oil. Sprinkle with the Parmesan and parsley. If desired, serve with marinara for dipping.

PER SERVING: **1 knot** · CALORIES **85** · FAT **1.5 g** · SATURATED FAT **0.5 g** · CHOLESTEROL **3 mg** · CARBOHYDRATE **14 g** · FIBER **0.5 g** · PROTEIN **5 g** · SUGARS **1 g** · SODIUM **256 mg**

skinny scoop

- To make the knots gluten-free, you can use Cup4Cup flour and increase the bake time by 5 minutes. The dough will be a different texture and more difficult to shape into knots, so just roll them into breadsticks instead.
- I used Fage and Stonyfield when testing this recipe and they worked perfectly; Chobani yogurt or another brand may result in sticky dough.

Q
V
GF

Fried Pickle Chips
with Cajun Buttermilk Ranch

Fried pickles are really popular in the South, so naturally, being from New York, I didn't discover them until I was an adult. Who would have thought that pickles could taste so good fried?! Even better, these air-fried chips come out flavorful and crisp without all the oil. They're a delicious accompaniment to a burger or a sandwich or perfect served as a fun, unique appetizer. Don't forget to serve them with Cajun buttermilk ranch dressing for dipping!

24 dill pickle slices

⅓ cup panko bread crumbs, regular or gluten-free

2 tablespoons cornmeal

1 teaspoon salt-free Cajun seasoning (I like the Spice Hunter)

1 tablespoon dried parsley

1 large egg, beaten

Olive oil spray

CAJUN BUTTERMILK RANCH DRESSING

⅓ cup 1% buttermilk

3 tablespoons light mayonnaise

3 tablespoons chopped scallion

¾ teaspoon salt-free Cajun seasoning

⅛ teaspoon garlic powder

⅛ teaspoon onion powder

⅛ teaspoon dried parsley

⅛ teaspoon kosher salt

Freshly ground black pepper

Place the pickles on paper towels to absorb the excess liquid, then pat dry (so the chips don't come out soggy).

In a medium bowl, combine the panko, cornmeal, Cajun seasoning, and parsley. Put the egg in a separate small bowl.

Working with one at a time, coat a pickle chip in the egg, then in the crumb mixture, gently pressing to adhere. Set aside on a work surface and repeat with the remaining pickles. Spray both sides of the pickles with oil.

Preheat the air fryer to 400°F.

Working in batches, arrange a single layer of the chips in the air fryer basket. Cook for 8 minutes, flipping halfway, until golden and crisp. (For a toaster oven–style air fryer, cook at 375°F; the timing remains the same.)

Meanwhile, for the dressing: In a small bowl, whisk together the buttermilk, mayonnaise, scallion, Cajun seasoning, garlic powder, onion powder, dried parsley, salt, and pepper to taste. Serve alongside the pickles for dipping.

PER SERVING: 6 chips + 2 tablespoons dressing · CALORIES 99 · FAT 5.5 g · SATURATED FAT 1 g · CHOLESTEROL 51 mg · CARBOHYDRATE 10 g · FIBER 1 g · PROTEIN 3 g · SUGARS 2 g · SODIUM 529 mg

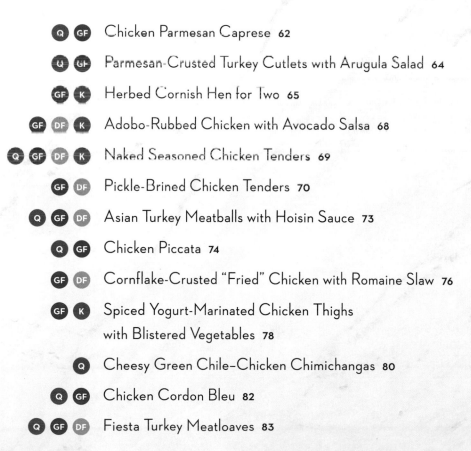

POULTRY

Q

GF

Chicken Parmesan Caprese

Two of my favorite dishes—chicken Parmesan and caprese salad—are combined in this fun spin on classic chicken Parm! The roasted cherry tomatoes and fresh basil give the dish a fresh twist and, it's all finished with a drizzle of tangy-sweet balsamic glaze.

TOMATOES

1 pint heirloom cherry tomatoes, halved

4 large garlic cloves, slightly smashed

1 teaspoon olive oil

¼ teaspoon kosher salt

¼ teaspoon freshly ground black pepper

CHICKEN

2 (8-ounce) boneless, skinless chicken breasts

½ teaspoon kosher salt

Freshly ground black pepper

1 tablespoon prepared pesto*

1 large egg, beaten

½ cup seasoned bread crumbs, whole wheat or gluten-free

2 tablespoons freshly grated Parmesan cheese

Olive oil spray

4 ounces fresh mozzarella cheese, thinly sliced

2 tablespoons balsamic glaze

Chopped fresh basil, for garnish

*Read the label to be sure this product is gluten-free.

Preheat the air fryer to 400°F.

For the tomatoes: In a medium bowl, combine the tomatoes, garlic, oil, salt, and pepper, tossing to coat. Transfer to the air fryer basket and cook for 4 to 5 minutes, shaking the basket a few times, until the tomatoes are soft. (For a toaster oven–style air fryer, the temperature remains the same; cook for 5 to 6 minutes.) Set the tomatoes aside and wipe out the basket with a paper towel.

Meanwhile, for the chicken: Halve each chicken breast horizontally to make a total of 4 cutlets. Place the chicken between two sheets of parchment paper or plastic wrap. Use a heavy skillet or meat mallet to pound to a ¼-inch thickness. Season both sides with the salt and pepper to taste and evenly coat with the pesto.

Place the egg in a shallow bowl. Combine the bread crumbs and Parmesan in a separate shallow bowl. Dip the chicken into the egg, then coat in the bread crumb mixture, gently pressing to adhere. Spray both sides with oil.

Preheat the air fryer to 400°F again.

Working in batches, place the chicken cutlets in the air fryer basket. Cook for 7 minutes, flipping halfway, until golden and cooked through. Top each cutlet with 1 ounce of the mozzarella and one-quarter of the tomatoes. Return the cutlets to the air fryer basket, in batches, and cook for about 2 minutes to melt the cheese. (For a toaster oven–style air fryer, the temperature remains the same; cook the chicken for 6 minutes and melt the cheese for 1 to 1½ minutes.) Remove from the air fryer, drizzle with the balsamic glaze, and top with the basil. Serve immediately.

PER SERVING: **1 cutlet** · CALORIES **364** · FAT **15.5 g** · SATURATED FAT **6 g** · CHOLESTEROL **144 mg** · CARBOHYDRATE **20 g** · FIBER **3 g** · PROTEIN **36 g** · SUGARS **10 g** · SODIUM **868 mg**

Parmesan-Crusted Turkey Cutlets with Arugula Salad

Thin meat cutlets breaded and fried, then topped with arugula and lemon is my favorite combination in the whole world. In fact, I'm known for ordering this when we eat out, even if it's not on the menu! These air-fried turkey cutlets come out just as delicious as the pan-fried ones, only so much lighter and healthier. If you can't find turkey cutlets, chicken or pork also work great.

4 turkey breast cutlets (18 ounces total)

Kosher salt and freshly ground black pepper

1 large egg, beaten

½ cup seasoned bread crumbs, regular or gluten-free

2 tablespoons grated Parmesan cheese

Olive oil spray

6 cups (4 ounces) baby arugula

1 tablespoon olive oil

1 tablespoon fresh lemon juice, plus 1 lemon cut into wedges for serving

Shaved Parmesan (optional)

One at a time, place a cutlet between two sheets of parchment paper or plastic wrap. Use a meat mallet or heavy skillet to pound to a ¼-inch thickness. Season the cutlets with ½ teaspoon salt (total) and pepper to taste.

Place the egg in a shallow medium bowl. In a separate bowl, combine the bread crumbs and Parmesan. Dip the turkey cutlets in the egg, then in the bread crumb mixture, gently pressing to adhere. Shake off the excess bread crumbs and place on a work surface. Spray both sides with oil.

Preheat the air fryer to 400°F.

Working in batches, place the turkey cutlets in the air fryer basket. Cook for about 8 minutes, flipping halfway, until golden brown and the center is cooked. (For a toaster oven–style air fryer, the temperature and timing remain the same.)

Place the arugula in a bowl and toss with the oil, lemon juice, ¼ teaspoon salt, and pepper to taste.

To serve, place a cutlet on each plate and top with 1½ cups arugula salad. Serve with lemon wedges, and top with some shaved Parmesan, if desired.

PER SERVING: 1 cutlet + 1½ cups salad · CALORIES 244 · FAT 6.5 g · SATURATED FAT 1.5 g · CHOLESTEROL 127 mg · CARBOHYDRATE 9 g · FIBER 1 g · PROTEIN 36 g · SUGARS 2 g · SODIUM 534 mg

GF
K

Herbed Cornish Hen for Two

Cornish hens may seem fussy to prepare, but cooking these little chickens is easier than you would imagine. When the occasion calls for an easy dinner for two, this delicious entrée fits the bill. Using the air fryer results in a beautifully browned hen that's moist, tender, and so flavorful. Plus, it takes only about 30 minutes. It pairs perfectly with a salad and roasted vegetables, such as asparagus, fennel, or Brussels sprouts. If you can't find the Cornish hen, you can substitute bone-in chicken breasts.

1 Cornish hen
    (about 2 pounds)

½ teaspoon ground cumin

½ teaspoon dried oregano

½ teaspoon garlic powder

½ teaspoon kosher salt

⅛ teaspoon freshly ground
    black pepper

1 teaspoon unsalted butter,
    melted

Discard the giblets from the hen or reserve for another use (they're great for stock!). Using kitchen shears, cut off the neck and along both sides of the backbone to remove. Trim any excess fat, then cut the hen in half along the breastbone. Trim off the wing tips.

In a small bowl, combine the cumin, oregano, garlic powder, salt, and pepper.

Place the hen skin side up on a work surface. Brush the skin with the melted butter, then season with the spices.

Preheat the air fryer to 380°F.

Transfer the hen to the air fryer basket, skin side down (both halves should fit in a 5.5 quart or larger size). Cook for about 30 minutes, flipping halfway, until golden and the internal temperature reaches 165°F. (For a toaster oven–style air fryer, the temperature and timing remain the same.) Tent with foil and let rest 5 minutes before serving.

skinny scoop To make this even lighter, remove the skin and you'll save around 250 calories and 25 grams of total fat per serving.

PER SERVING: 6½ ounces chicken, with skin · CALORIES 499 · FAT 35.5 g · SATURATED FAT 10.5 g · CHOLESTEROL 246 mg · CARBOHYDRATE 1 g · FIBER 0 g · PROTEIN 41 g · SUGARS 0 g · SODIUM 400 mg

GF
DF
K

Adobo-Rubbed Chicken with Avocado Salsa

With the help of an air fryer, tender and perfectly cooked chicken breasts are just a few simple (and dare I say foolproof?) steps away. First, brining the chicken in a solution of warm water and salt seasons the meat inside and out. Next, the spice rub gives the chicken a flavor-packed coating and beautiful color. Lastly, the air fryer does all the work, cooking it evenly and quickly! Use the chicken as a base for salads or in any recipe that requires cooked chicken, such as the chimichanga recipe on page 80.

CHICKEN

Kosher salt

4 (6-ounce) boneless, skinless chicken breasts

¾ teaspoon garlic powder

½ teaspoon onion powder

½ teaspoon ground cumin

½ teaspoon ancho chile powder

½ teaspoon sweet paprika

½ teaspoon dried oregano

⅛ teaspoon crushed red pepper flakes

Olive oil spray

AVOCADO SALSA

½ cup finely diced red onion

3 tablespoons fresh lime juice

10 ounces avocado (2 medium Hass), diced

1 tablespoon chopped fresh cilantro

Kosher salt

For the chicken: Fill a large bowl with lukewarm water and add ¼ cup salt. Stir to dissolve. Let the water cool to room temperature. Add the chicken to the water and refrigerate for at least 1 hour to brine. Remove the chicken from the water and pat dry with paper towels (discard the brine).

In a small bowl, combine ¾ teaspoon salt, the garlic powder, onion powder, cumin, ancho powder, paprika, oregano, and pepper flakes. Spritz the chicken all over with oil, then rub with the spice mix.

Preheat the air fryer to 380°F.

Working in batches, place the chicken breasts in the air fryer basket. Cook for about 10 minutes, flipping halfway, until browned and cooked through. (For a toaster oven–style air fryer, cook at 350°F; the timing remains the same.)

Meanwhile, for the avocado salsa: In a medium bowl, combine the onion and lime juice. Fold in the avocado and cilantro and season with ¼ teaspoon salt.

Serve the chicken topped with the salsa.

PER SERVING: **1 chicken breast + ½ cup salsa** · CALORIES **324** · FAT **15 g** SATURATED FAT **2.5 g** · CHOLESTEROL **109 mg** · CARBOHYDRATE **10 g** · FIBER **5.5 g** · PROTEIN **38 g** · SUGARS **2 g** · SODIUM **490 mg**

Q
GF
DF
K

Naked Seasoned Chicken Tenders

The trick to getting these chicken tenders so juicy is coating them with a little mayonnaise, which also helps the spices cling to the meat. They come out so tender and flavorful and are perfect for dinner with your favorite vegetables, served over salad, and even for meal prep. You can season the chicken with any combination of spices, too. Here, I use a slightly smoky spice mixture, but I also love this with salt, garlic powder, dried oregano, and Parmesan cheese for an Italian-inspired twist.

SEASONING

1 teaspoon kosher salt

½ teaspoon garlic powder

½ teaspoon onion powder

½ teaspoon chili powder*

¼ teaspoon sweet paprika

¼ teaspoon freshly ground black pepper

CHICKEN

8 chicken breast tenders (1 pound total)

2 tablespoons mayonnaise

*Read the label to be sure this product is gluten-free.

For the seasoning: In a small bowl, combine the salt, garlic powder, onion powder, chili powder, paprika, and pepper.

For the chicken: Place the chicken in a medium bowl and add the mayonnaise. Mix well to coat all over, then sprinkle with the seasoning mix.

Preheat the air fryer to 375°F.

Working in batches, arrange a single layer of the chicken in the air fryer basket. Cook for 6 to 7 minutes, flipping halfway, until cooked through in the center. (For a toaster oven-style air fryer, the temperature and timing remain the same.) Serve immediately.

PER SERVING: **2 tenders** · CALORIES **183** · FAT **8.5 g** · SATURATED FAT **1.5 g** · CHOLESTEROL **75 mg** · CARBOHYDRATE **0 g** · FIBER **0 g** · PROTEIN **24 g** · SUGARS **0 g** · SODIUM **457 mg**

GF
DF

Pickle-Brined Chicken Tenders

Madison absolutely *loves* pickles. I'm not exaggerating when I say that we go through several jars of them each month. We don't let all that leftover pickle juice go to waste though—it turns into an amazing brine for these crispy chicken fingers, making the meat super juicy and tender.

12 chicken tenders
(1¼ pounds total)

1¼ cups dill pickle juice,
plus more if needed

1 large egg

1 large egg white

½ teaspoon kosher salt

Freshly ground black pepper

½ cup seasoned bread
crumbs, regular or
gluten-free

½ cup seasoned panko
bread crumbs, regular or
gluten-free

Olive oil spray

Place the chicken in a shallow bowl and cover with the pickle juice (enough to cover completely). Cover and marinate for 8 hours in the refrigerator.

Drain the chicken and pat completely dry with paper towels (discard the marinade).

In a medium bowl, beat together the whole egg, egg white, salt, and pepper to taste. In a shallow bowl, combine both bread crumbs.

Working with one piece at a time, dip the chicken in the egg mixture, then into the bread crumbs, gently pressing to adhere. Shake off any excess bread crumbs and place on a work surface. Generously spray both sides of the chicken with oil.

Preheat the air fryer to 400°F.

Working in batches, arrange a single layer of the chicken in the air fryer basket. Cook for 10 to 12 minutes, flipping halfway, until cooked through, crispy, and golden. (For a toaster oven-style air fryer, the temperature remains the same; cook for about 10 minutes.) Serve immediately.

PER SERVING: **3 tenders** · CALORIES **257** · FAT **5.5 g** · SATURATED FAT **1.5 g** · CHOLESTEROL **137 mg** · CARBOHYDRATE **14 g** · FIBER **1 g** · PROTEIN **35 g** · SUGARS **1 g** · SODIUM **742 mg**

Q
GF
DF

Asian Turkey Meatballs with Hoisin Sauce

These zesty turkey meatballs are packed with so much flavor from the cilantro, scallions, ginger, garlic, soy sauce, and sesame oil, but the drizzle of sweet-savory hoisin sauce takes it to the next level! They're perfect as a main course served over brown rice, spiralized zucchini, or cauliflower rice, or for easy party food, served as an appetizer with toothpicks.

MEATBALLS

1⅓ pounds 93% lean ground turkey

¼ cup panko bread crumbs, regular or gluten-free

3 chopped scallions, plus more for garnish

¼ cup chopped fresh cilantro

1 large egg

1 tablespoon grated fresh ginger

1 garlic clove, minced

1 tablespoon reduced-sodium soy sauce* or tamari

2 teaspoons toasted sesame oil

¾ teaspoon kosher salt

Olive oil spray

HOISIN SAUCE

2 tablespoons hoisin sauce*

2 tablespoons fresh orange juice

1 tablespoon reduced-sodium soy sauce* or tamari

*Read the label to be sure this product is gluten-free.

For the meatballs: In a large bowl, combine the ground turkey, panko, scallions, cilantro, egg, ginger, garlic, soy sauce, sesame oil, and salt. Gently mix with your hands until thoroughly combined. Roll into 12 meatballs (¼ cup each) and spritz with oil.

Preheat the air fryer to 380°F.

Working in batches, arrange a single layer of the meatballs in the air fryer basket. Cook for about 9 minutes, flipping halfway, until cooked through in the center and browned. (For a toaster oven–style air fryer, cook at 350°F for about 12 minutes.)

Meanwhile, for the hoisin sauce: In a small saucepan, combine the hoisin sauce, orange juice, and soy sauce and bring to a boil over medium-low heat. Reduce the heat to low and cook until the sauce is reduced slightly, 2 to 3 minutes.

Drizzle the meatballs with the sauce and serve topped with scallions.

PER SERVING: **3 meatballs** • CALORIES **313** • FAT **16.5 g** • SATURATED FAT **4 g** • CHOLESTEROL **158 mg** • CARBOHYDRATE **10 g** • FIBER **1 g** • PROTEIN **31 g** • SUGARS **4 g** • SODIUM **755 mg**

Q

GF

Chicken Piccata

Chicken piccata is a classic Italian dish. Traditionally, the chicken is coated in flour and pan-fried in lots of butter and oil. This version, inspired by Ina Garten's recipe, is made with breaded cutlets (using bread crumbs instead of flour, which my family actually prefers). They're air-fried until golden and crisp, then topped with a lemony pan sauce made with white wine and capers. It's lighter in calories, but not in taste!

CHICKEN

2 (8-ounce) boneless, skinless chicken breasts, all fat trimmed

¼ teaspoon kosher salt

Freshly ground black pepper

2 large egg whites

⅔ cup seasoned bread crumbs, whole wheat or gluten-free

Olive oil spray

SAUCE

1 tablespoon whipped butter

½ cup reduced-sodium chicken broth*

¼ cup dry white wine

Juice of 1 lemon, lemon halves reserved

Freshly ground black pepper

1 tablespoon capers, drained

FOR SERVING

1 lemon, sliced

Chopped fresh parsley leaves

For the chicken: Halve the chicken breasts horizontally for a total of 4 cutlets. Place the cutlets between two sheets of parchment paper or plastic wrap. Use a heavy skillet or meat mallet to pound to a ¼-inch thickness. Season both sides with the salt and pepper to taste.

In a shallow bowl, beat the egg whites with 1 teaspoon water. Place the bread crumbs on a large plate. Dip each piece of chicken in the egg, then in the bread crumbs, gently pressing to adhere. Shake off any excess bread crumbs and place on a work surface. Generously spray both sides of the chicken with olive oil.

Preheat the air fryer to 370°F.

Working in batches, place the chicken cutlets in the air fryer. Cook for about 6 minutes, flipping halfway, until cooked through, crisp, and golden. (For a toaster oven–style air fryer, cook at 350°F for 5 minutes.)

Meanwhile, for the sauce: In a medium skillet, melt the butter over medium heat. Add the chicken broth, wine, lemon juice, reserved lemon halves, and pepper to taste. Boil over high heat until the liquid is reduced by half, 3 to 4 minutes. Remove from the heat. Discard the lemon halves and stir in the capers.

To serve: Divide the chicken among serving plates. Spoon 2 tablespoons of the sauce over each piece of chicken. Top with the lemon slices and parsley and serve.

*Read the label to be sure this product is gluten-free.

PER SERVING: **1 chicken cutlet + 2 tablespoons sauce** · CALORIES **232** · FAT **6 g** · SATURATED FAT **2 g** · CHOLESTEROL **78 mg** · CARBOHYDRATE **13 g** · FIBER **2 g** · PROTEIN **29 g** · SUGARS **2 g** · SODIUM **691 mg**

Cornflake-Crusted "Fried" Chicken with Romaine Slaw

These crisp, cornflake-coated drumsticks are a throwback to childhood! You can pretty much bread chicken in anything that crumbles—pretzels, tortilla chips, gluten-free rice crackers, matzo, you name it! But nothing brings back memories like cornflake-crusted chicken. Mom would leave the skin on the chicken, but to keep this dish low-cal, I take it off. Trust me, you won't miss it. Feel free to experiment with your own crunchy-coating combos.

CHICKEN

8 bone-in chicken drumsticks (30 ounces total), skin removed

½ teaspoon kosher salt

2 large eggs

½ teaspoon sweet paprika

¼ teaspoon garlic powder

¼ teaspoon chili powder*

Olive oil spray

CRUMB COATING

1⅔ cups (3½ ounces) regular or gluten-free cornflakes

Olive oil spray

1 teaspoon kosher salt

1 tablespoon dried parsley

1½ teaspoons sweet paprika

1 teaspoon dried marjoram

1 teaspoon dried thyme

½ teaspoon garlic powder

½ teaspoon onion powder

¼ teaspoon chili powder*

Romaine Slaw (recipe follows), for serving

*Read the label to be sure this product is gluten-free.

For the chicken: Season the chicken with the salt. In a shallow bowl, beat the eggs with 1 teaspoon water, the paprika, garlic powder, and chili powder. Set aside.

For the crumb coating: Place the cornflakes in a gallon zip-top bag and crush with a rolling pin or the bottom of a cup, keeping the pieces a bit chunky. Transfer to a shallow bowl. Spritz the cornflakes with a little oil (this helps the seasoning stick to the cornflakes), then add the salt, parsley, paprika, marjoram, thyme, garlic powder, onion powder, and chili powder. Mix well to combine.

Working with one at a time, dip each drumstick in the egg mix, then in the crumbs, pressing to coat completely. Transfer to a work surface and spray with oil on all sides.

Preheat the air fryer to 350°F.

Working in batches, arrange a single layer of the chicken in the air fryer basket. Cook for about 28 minutes, flipping halfway, until the chicken is cooked through and the coating is golden. (For a toaster oven–style air fryer, cook at 300°F for 34 to 36 minutes.) Let cool for 5 minutes before serving with the slaw.

Romaine Slaw

SERVES 4

5 cups shredded romaine lettuce

¼ cup slivered red onion

1½ tablespoons olive oil

1½ tablespoons apple cider vinegar

4 teaspoons fresh lime juice

¼ teaspoon kosher salt

Freshly ground black pepper

In a large bowl, combine the lettuce, onion, oil, vinegar, lime juice, salt, and pepper to taste. Toss well and serve right away.

PER SERVING: 1¼ cups · CALORIES 60 · FAT 5 g · SATURATED FAT 0.5 g · CHOLESTEROL 0 mg · CARBOHYDRATE 3 g · FIBER 1.5 g · PROTEIN 1 g · SUGARS 1 g · SODIUM 76 mg

PER SERVING: 2 drumsticks · CALORIES 346 · FAT 11 g · SATURATED FAT 3 g · CHOLESTEROL 284 mg · CARBOHYDRATE 15 g · FIBER 1 g · PROTEIN 45 g · SUGARS 2 g · SODIUM 693 mg

GF

K

Spiced Yogurt-Marinated Chicken Thighs with Blistered Vegetables

If you've never had tandoori chicken before, prepare to fall in love! This technique was one of my favorites in *Skinnytaste One & Done*, and who knew that you could do tandoori-style chicken in the air fryer, too? The meat chars up beautifully, and since it ended up being one of my favorite things I developed for this book, I just couldn't leave it out! Here, I used boneless chicken thighs, which are so easy. Shishito peppers are not Indian, but they pair perfectly with the chicken and charred tomatoes. If you wish, you can serve naan bread or brown basmati rice on the side.

¼ cup whole-milk yogurt (not Greek)

3 garlic cloves, minced

2 tablespoons fresh lemon juice

1 teaspoon grated fresh ginger

1 teaspoon garam masala*

¼ teaspoon ground turmeric

¼ teaspoon cayenne pepper

1¼ teaspoons kosher salt

8 (4-ounce) boneless, skinless chicken thighs, trimmed

7 ounces shishito peppers

2 medium vine tomatoes, quartered

Olive oil spray

1 tablespoon chopped fresh cilantro, for garnish

1 lemon, cut into wedges

*Read the label to be sure this product is gluten-free.

In a small bowl, stir together the yogurt, garlic, lemon juice, ginger, garam masala, turmeric, cayenne, and 1 teaspoon of the salt. Place the chicken thighs in a large zip-top bag and add the marinade to coat. Marinate the chicken in the refrigerator for at least 2 hours, or overnight.

Preheat the air fryer to 400°F.

Remove the chicken from the marinade (discard the marinade). Working in batches, arrange a single layer of the chicken in the air fryer basket. Cook for about 14 minutes, flipping halfway, until slightly browned and cooked through. (For a toaster oven–style air fryer, the temperature and timing remain the same.) Set the cooked chicken aside and tent with foil.

Spritz the shishitos and tomatoes all over with oil. Transfer to the air fryer basket and cook for 8 minutes, shaking halfway, until soft and slightly charred. (For a toaster oven–style air fryer, the temperature and timing remain the same.) Sprinkle with the remaining ¼ teaspoon salt.

Transfer the chicken and vegetables to plates. Garnish with cilantro and serve with the lemon wedges on the side.

PER SERVING: 2 thighs + one-quarter of the vegetables · CALORIES 321 · FAT 10 g · SATURATED FAT 2.5 g · CHOLESTEROL 218 mg · CARBOHYDRATE 11 g · FIBER 2 g · PROTEIN 46 g · SUGARS 5 g · SODIUM 563 mg

Q

Cheesy Green Chile–Chicken Chimichangas

Chimichangas, deep-fried burritos popular in Tex-Mex cuisine, are seriously delicious, but usually dripping in grease and loaded with calories. These lighter chicken, green chile, and pepper Jack cheese chimichangas are a much healthier twist on the classic. To simplify the recipe for a quick weeknight meal, I used the breast of a cooked rotisserie chicken.

PICO DE GALLO

½ cup diced tomato

3 tablespoons chopped onion

1 tablespoon chopped fresh cilantro, plus more for garnish

1 teaspoon fresh lime juice

¼ teaspoon kosher salt

Freshly ground black pepper

CHIMICHANGAS

12 ounces shredded leftover or rotisserie chicken breast

Juice of ½ navel orange

Juice of ½ lime

1 large garlic clove, minced

1 teaspoon ground cumin

1 (4-ounce) can mild diced green chiles, drained

4 (7- to 8-inch) low-carb whole wheat tortillas (I used La Tortilla Factory)

½ cup (2 ounces) shredded pepper Jack cheese

Olive oil spray

FOR SERVING

3 cups shredded lettuce

4 tablespoons sour cream

4 ounces avocado (from 1 small Hass), diced

For the pico de gallo: In a small bowl, combine the tomato, onion, cilantro, lime juice, salt, and pepper to taste.

For the chimichangas: In a large bowl, combine the chicken, orange juice, lime juice, garlic, cumin, and drained chiles. Mix well to incorporate.

On a work surface, working with one at a time, place one-quarter of the chicken mixture (almost ¾ cup) onto the bottom third of a tortilla. Sprinkle each with 2 tablespoons cheese. Lift the edge nearest you and wrap it around the filling. Fold the left and right sides in toward the center and continue to roll into a tight cylinder. Set aside, seam side down, and repeat with the remaining tortillas and filling.

Preheat the air fryer to 400°F.

Lightly spray all sides of the chimichangas with oil. Place 2 of the chimichangas seam side down in the air fryer basket. (Make sure each chimichanga is tightly wrapped and seam side down in the basket or it will open during cooking.) Cook for 7 to 8 minutes, flipping halfway, until golden and crisp. (For a toaster oven–style air fryer, cook at 350°F; the timing remains the same.) Repeat with the remaining chimichangas.

To serve: Place ¾ cup shredded lettuce on each plate. Place a chimichanga on top, along with 2 tablespoons pico de gallo, 1 tablespoon sour cream, and 1 ounce avocado. Garnish with cilantro. Serve immediately.

skinny scoop It's finished with a dollop of sour cream, pico de gallo, and avocado, but to make it an even fuller meal, you can serve the chimichangas with a side of rice or refried beans.

PER SERVING: 1 chimichanga + ¾ cup lettuce + toppings · CALORIES 391 · FAT 18.5 g · SATURATED FAT 6 g · CHOLESTEROL 93 mg · CARBOHYDRATE 30 g · FIBER 16.5 g · PROTEIN 40 g · SUGARS 5 g · SODIUM 716 mg

Q
GF

Chicken Cordon Bleu

When I was growing up, my mom used to make this family-friendly dish for dinner all the time, and it was always a favorite—Mom, however, didn't have an air fryer, so she deep-fried them. This healthier version tastes just as good as hers (with a lot less calories and fat!), and is perfect with a crisp green salad on the side.

8 (4 ounces each) thin-sliced chicken breast cutlets

¾ teaspoon kosher salt

Freshly ground black pepper

4 slices (1 ounce each) reduced-sodium deli ham, halved lengthwise

4 slices (1 ounce each) low-sodium Swiss cheese (such as Boar's Head Lacey), halved lengthwise

1 large egg

2 large egg whites

¾ cup bread crumbs, regular or gluten-free

2 tablespoons grated Parmesan cheese

Olive oil spray

Season the chicken cutlets with ¾ teaspoon salt and pepper to taste. Working with one at a time, place a cutlet on a work surface and put a half-slice of ham and cheese on top. Roll the chicken up, then set aside, seam side down. Repeat with the remaining chicken, ham, and cheese.

In a shallow bowl, beat together the whole egg and egg whites. In a separate shallow bowl, combine the bread crumbs and Parmesan.

Dip the chicken into the egg mixture, then into the bread crumbs, gently pressing to adhere. Spray both sides with oil.

Preheat the air fryer to 400°F.

Working in batches, place chicken rolls seam side down in the air fryer basket. Cook for 12 minutes, flipping halfway, until golden and cooked through. (For a toaster oven–style air fryer, cook at 350°F; the timing remains the same.) Serve immediately.

skinny scoop The trick to easily rolling the chicken is using superthin cutlets. If your cutlets are giving you trouble, pound them to make them thinner—no more than ¼ inch thick.

PER SERVING: **2 rolls** • CALORIES **497** • FAT **15.5 g** • SATURATED FAT **6.5 g** • CHOLESTEROL **222 mg** • CARBOHYDRATE **16 g** • FIBER **1 g** • PROTEIN **69 g** • SUGARS **2 g** • SODIUM **983 mg**

Q
GF
DF

Fiesta Turkey Meatloaves

I give traditional meatloaf a Mexican touch by adding black beans, corn, and salsa. Shaping them into individual patties helps them cook very fast. If you want to make them spicy, add some chopped jalapeños or chipotle sauce to the mixture.

MEATLOAVES

1 pound 93% lean ground turkey

⅓ cup bread crumbs, regular or gluten-free

⅓ cup canned black beans, rinsed and drained

⅓ cup frozen corn

¼ cup jarred chunky mild salsa

¼ cup minced onion

¼ cup chopped scallions

2 tablespoons chopped fresh cilantro

1 large egg, beaten

1 tablespoon tomato paste

1 teaspoon kosher salt

½ teaspoon ground cumin

GLAZE

2 tablespoons ketchup

2 tablespoons jarred mild salsa

For the meatloaves: In a medium bowl, combine the turkey, bread crumbs, beans, corn, salsa, onion, scallions, cilantro, egg, tomato paste, salt, and cumin and mix well. Divide the mixture into 4 equal portions and shape into 1-inch-thick round patties.

For the glaze: In a small bowl, stir together the ketchup and salsa.

Preheat the air fryer to 350°F.

Working in batches, place the meatloaves in the air fryer basket. Cook for about 18 minutes, flipping halfway, until the center is cooked through. Brush the meatloaves with the glaze and return to the air fryer and cook for about 2 minutes to heat through. (For a toaster oven–style air fryer, cook at 325°F; the timing remains the same.) Serve immediately.

skinny scoop You can toss the remaining beans from the can with 1⅓ cups thawed corn, 1 chopped tomato, lime juice, cilantro, and salt to make a salsa on the side.

PER SERVING: **1 loaf** · CALORIES **279** · FAT **11.5 g** · SATURATED FAT **3 g** · CHOLESTEROL **130 mg** · CARBOHYDRATE **18 g** · FIBER **3 g** · PROTEIN **26 g** · SUGARS **4 g** · SODIUM **695 mg**

BEEF, PORK & LAMB

Q
GF
K

Low-Carb Cheeseburger Sliders with Special Sauce

Man, cheeseburgers are so dang delicious that even when I'm watching my waistline, I can't deny myself one! That's when these lettuce-wrapped babies make an appearance. No bun, no problem! The meat is mixed with cheese, air-fried to perfection, then topped with tomatoes, red onion, pickles, and a mouthwatering "special sauce." Trust me, you won't even miss the bun. They taste just like summer, only there's no grill required, so you can enjoy them year-round.

SLIDERS

1 pound 90% lean ground beef

¼ cup (1 ounce) shredded reduced-fat cheddar cheese*

1 tablespoon yellow mustard

¾ teaspoon kosher salt

¼ teaspoon onion powder

⅛ teaspoon freshly ground black pepper

SPECIAL SAUCE

2 tablespoons light mayonnaise

2 teaspoons ketchup

½ teaspoon yellow mustard

½ teaspoon dill pickle juice

⅛ teaspoon onion powder

⅛ teaspoon garlic powder

⅛ teaspoon sweet paprika

FOR SERVING

4 large outer leaves iceberg lettuce, each halved lengthwise

8 (¼-inch-thick) slices tomato (from 2 small)

2 slices red onion (from 1 small), rings separated

8 dill pickle chips

*Read the label to be sure this product is gluten-free.

For the sliders: In a large bowl, combine the beef, cheddar, mustard, salt, onion powder, and pepper. Gently form the meat into 8 equal patties, about ½ inch thick. Press your finger in the center of each patty to create a dimple (this will help maintain their flat shape when they cook).

For the special sauce: In a medium bowl, combine the mayonnaise, ketchup, mustard, pickle juice, onion powder, garlic powder, and paprika and mix until smooth.

Preheat the air fryer to 400°F.

PER SERVING: **2 sliders** · CALORIES **271** · FAT **15.5 g** · SATURATED FAT **6 g** · CHOLESTEROL **81 mg** · CARBOHYDRATE **6 g** · FIBER **1.5 g** · PROTEIN **26 g** · SUGARS **3 g** · SODIUM **585 mg**

Working in batches, arrange a single layer of sliders in the air fryer basket. Cook, flipping halfway, to your desired doneness, 8 minutes for medium. (For a toaster oven–style air fryer, the temperature and timing remain the same.)

To serve: Place 2 lettuce halves on each plate and top each with a slice of tomato, a slider, onion, special sauce, and pickles. Serve immediately.

Roast Beef with Horseradish-Chive Cream

Roast beef: It's a dish loved by all in my family. I typically make it only on weekends though because of its long roasting time. But the air fryer has really switched things up in my house—you can now make a perfectly juicy, medium-rare roast beef in just 30 minutes—total game changer! And leftovers are perfect for roast beef sandwiches. Serve it with roasted veggies, cauliflower mash, or a big salad on the side.

BEEF

1 (2-pound) trimmed top round roast, tied

1 teaspoon kosher salt

1 teaspoon olive oil

1 tablespoon Dijon mustard

1 teaspoon prepared horseradish

1 garlic clove, minced

HORSERADISH-CHIVE CREAM

⅔ cup sour cream

2¼ tablespoons prepared horseradish

2¼ tablespoons Dijon mustard

1 tablespoon minced chives

¼ teaspoon kosher salt

Freshly ground black pepper

For the beef: Remove the roast from the refrigerator and let come to room temperature, about 1 hour. Pat dry with paper towels. Season with the salt.

In a small bowl, combine the oil, mustard, horseradish, and garlic. Rub the outside of the roast with the mixture.

Preheat the air fryer to 325°F.

Place the roast in the air fryer basket. Cook for 30 to 35 minutes, flipping halfway, until browned and a thermometer inserted in the center reads 125° to 130°F for medium rare. (For a toaster oven–style air fryer, cook at 300°F for 25 to 30 minutes.)

Meanwhile, for the horseradish-chive cream: In a medium bowl, combine the sour cream, horseradish, mustard, chives, salt, and pepper to taste and mix until smooth. Refrigerate until ready to use.

Transfer the roast to a cutting board, tent with foil, and let rest for 10 to 15 minutes before carving. Thinly slice and serve with the horseradish cream on the side.

skinny scoop: If you don't have time to let the roast come to room temperature before you cook it, add about 5 minutes to the cook time. Larger roasts will require more time in the air fryer.

PER SERVING: 3 ounces beef + 2 tablespoons sauce · CALORIES 275 · FAT 18.5 g · SATURATED FAT 6.5 g · CHOLESTEROL 88 mg · CARBOHYDRATE 2 g · FIBER 0 g · PROTEIN 24 g · SUGARS 1 g · SODIUM 458 mg

Q

GF

K

Carne Asada Salad

I love steak. It's by far one of my favorite things to cook when I want something *quick* that everyone in my house will love. I usually serve my steak with a salad on the side, or turn it into a big salad as I did here.

GUACAMOLE

1 small Hass avocado (4 ounces)

¼ cup diced tomato

2 tablespoons diced red onion

2 teaspoons chopped fresh cilantro

2 teaspoons fresh lime juice

½ teaspoon kosher salt

Freshly ground black pepper

STEAK

10 ounces top sirloin steak (½ to ¾ inch thick)

1 large garlic clove, minced

½ teaspoon kosher salt

1 teaspoon ground cumin

Freshly ground black pepper

¼ lime

FOR SERVING

3 cups chopped romaine lettuce

¼ cup (1 ounce) shredded Monterey Jack cheese

½ cup pico de gallo, store-bought or homemade (see the chimichanga recipe, page 80)

1 jalapeño, sliced thin (optional)

Lime wedges

For the guacamole: In a small bowl, mash the avocado, then add the tomato, red onion, cilantro, lime juice, salt, and pepper to taste. Mix and set aside.

For the steak: Season the steak with the garlic, salt, cumin, and pepper to taste.

Preheat the air fryer to 400°F.

Place the steak in the air fryer basket. Cook, flipping halfway, until cooked to your desired doneness, 7 to 10 minutes for medium, depending on the thickness of your steak. (For a toaster oven–style air fryer, the temperature and timing remain the same.) Let the steak rest for 5 minutes.

Squeeze the lime juice over the steak and thinly slice.

To serve: Place 1½ cups lettuce, 2 tablespoons cheese, and ¼ cup guacamole on each plate. Top with half of the steak slices, ¼ cup pico de gallo, and jalapeño (if using). Serve with lime wedges on the side.

PER SERVING: **1 salad** · CALORIES **388** · FAT **22 g** · SATURATED FAT **6.5 g** · CHOLESTEROL **108 mg** · CARBOHYDRATE **16 g** · FIBER **7.5 g** · PROTEIN **37 g** · SUGARS **4 g** · SODIUM **994 mg**

Soy-Sesame Marinated Flank Steak

It always blows my mind that you can make a perfectly cooked medium-rare steak in the air fryer without smoking up the whole kitchen! This recipe uses flank steak, a very lean primal cut that really benefits from marinating overnight. Soy sauce is loaded with flavor compounds that convey savoriness or umami, making it a potent base for the marinade. It's important to slice this lean cut very thinly across the grain so it's not tough. Although it may seem like I'm using a lot of oil and sugar, keep in mind that most of the marinade gets tossed before cooking.

6 tablespoons reduced-sodium soy sauce* or tamari

2 tablespoons toasted sesame oil

2 tablespoons sugar

1 tablespoon grated fresh ginger

1 shallot, minced

1 garlic clove, minced

¼ teaspoon crushed red pepper flakes

1½ pounds flank steak

1 scallion, thinly sliced

Toasted sesame seeds, for topping

*Read the label to be sure this product is gluten-free.

In a large bowl, combine the soy sauce, sesame oil, sugar, ginger, shallot, garlic, and pepper flakes and mix until the sugar dissolves. Add the steak and massage the marinade into the meat. Cover with plastic wrap and let marinate overnight in the refrigerator.

Preheat the air fryer to 400°F.

Remove the steak from the marinade (discard the marinade). Working in two batches if needed, place the steak in the air fryer basket. Cook, flipping halfway, until charred on the outside and cooked to your desired doneness, about 12 minutes for medium rare. (For a toaster oven–style air fryer, the temperature and timing remain the same.)

Let rest for 5 minutes before very thinly slicing across the grain. Transfer to a platter. Serve topped with the scallion and sesame seeds.

skinny scoop If the steak is too large for your air fryer, cut it into two pieces.

PER SERVING: 4½ ounces steak · CALORIES 287 · FAT 13 g · SATURATED FAT 4.5 g · CHOLESTEROL 117 mg · CARBOHYDRATE 3 g · FIBER 0.5 g · PROTEIN 38 g · SUGARS 2 g · SODIUM 298 mg

Korean Pork Lettuce Wraps

The inspiration for this dish came from *bo ssam*, a Korean dish typically made with pork belly and served with lettuce wraps. My friend John Chan used to make *bo ssam* at every BBQ and it was always a hit. Here, I used a leaner cut, pork tenderloin, which I sliced and marinated overnight, and simplified the dipping sauce. You don't need a grill to make these, since the air fryer lets you do it any time of the year!

PORK

1 pound pork tenderloin, cut into 12 (½-inch-thick) slices

¼ teaspoon kosher salt

⅛ teaspoon freshly ground black pepper

3 scallions, chopped

3 garlic cloves, crushed

¼ cup reduced-sodium soy sauce

1 tablespoon gochujang

1 tablespoon light brown sugar

1 tablespoon grated fresh ginger

GOCHUJANG SAUCE

2 tablespoons gochujang

2 tablespoons mirin

1 teaspoon toasted sesame oil

FOR SERVING

2¼ cups cooked brown rice

12 baby romaine or green leaf lettuce leaves

½ tablespoon sesame seeds

2 scallions, sliced

For the pork: Place the pork slices in a large bowl and season with the salt and pepper. In a small bowl, combine the scallions, garlic, soy sauce, gochujang, brown sugar, and ginger and mix well. Pour over the pork and toss to coat. Cover with plastic wrap and marinate in the refrigerator overnight.

Preheat the air fryer to 400°F.

Working in batches, arrange a single layer of pork (discarding the excess marinade) in the air fryer. Cook for about 10 minutes, flipping halfway, until browned and no longer pink in the center. (For a toaster oven–style air fryer, the temperature and timing remain the same.)

For the gochujang sauce: In a small bowl, combine the gochujang, mirin, and sesame oil and mix until smooth.

To serve: Place 3 tablespoons brown rice on each lettuce leaf. Top with a slice of pork, 1 teaspoon of the gochujang sauce, and some of the sesame seeds and scallions. Wrap the leaves over the rice and pork into little burrito-like bundles and eat right away.

PER SERVING: **3 lettuce wraps** • CALORIES **311** • FAT **5 g** • SATURATED FAT **1 g** • CHOLESTEROL **74 mg** • CARBOHYDRATE **34 g** • FIBER **3.5 g** • PROTEIN **28 g** • SUGARS **6 g** • SODIUM **398 mg**

Q
GF
K

Meat Lovers' Pizza-Stuffed Peppers

Two of Tommy's favorite foods—pizza and stuffed peppers—combined in one dish! These peppers are stuffed with the same toppings you would put on a pizza, but without all the carbs. They make a delicious lunch or light dinner served with a big salad on the side. Here, I filled them with sausage, pepperoni, and cheese, but if you want to go vegetarian, swap the meat for sliced mushrooms, basil, or whatever you like on your pizza!

1 (2.8-ounce) link sweet Italian pork sausage*

4 medium bell peppers

Olive oil spray

1 cup marinara sauce

1½ cups (6 ounces) shredded mozzarella cheese

12 slices turkey pepperoni, halved

*Read the label to be sure this product Is gluten-free.

Preheat the air fryer to 370°F.

Place the sausage in the air fryer basket and cook for 10 minutes, flipping halfway, until cooked through. (For a toaster oven-style air fryer, cook at 350°F; the timing remains the same.) Set aside to cool, then chop into small pieces.

Halve the peppers lengthwise and remove the seeds. Spray both sides with oil.

Reduce the air fryer temperature to 350°F.

Place the peppers in the air fryer basket and cook for 6 to 8 minutes, flipping halfway, until slightly softened. (For a toaster oven-style air fryer, the temperature remains the same; cook for 6 minutes.) Transfer to a plate.

Fill each pepper half with 2 tablespoons marinara and top with 3 tablespoons mozzarella, a few pieces of sausage, and 3 pepperoni halves.

Working in batches, return the stuffed peppers in a single layer to the air fryer. Cook for 6 to 7 minutes, until the cheese is melted and the sauce is hot. (For a toaster oven-style air fryer, the temperature remains the same; cook for about 5 minutes.) Serve immediately.

PER SERVING: **2 pepper halves** · CALORIES **257** · FAT **15 g** · SATURATED FAT **7.5 g** · CHOLESTEROL **54 mg** · CARBOHYDRATE **13 g** · FIBER **3.5 g** · PROTEIN **17 g** · SUGARS **7 g** · SODIUM **658 mg**

Q
GF
DF

Breaded Pork Cutlets
with Avocado, Tomatoes, and Lime

Seriously, this is one of my family's favorite weeknight recipes! My husband requests these cutlets all the time, and my sister-in-law even started making them for my picky niece (we just tell her it's chicken!). What makes them so special: The pork is pounded thin, like a chicken cutlet, and the sazón seasoning delivers so much flavor. The lime wedges, of course, are a must to squeeze over the meat just before eating. We serve the cutlets with tomatoes and avocado on the side, or when Tommy's really good, I make it with rice and beans (his favorite!).

8 thin boneless pork loin cutlets (about 3 ounces each), trimmed of excess fat

¾ teaspoon adobo seasoning salt

1 large egg, beaten

1 teaspoon sazón seasoning (I like Badia)

½ cup plus 2 tablespoons seasoned bread crumbs, regular or gluten-free

Olive oil spray

5 ounces avocado (from 1 medium Hass), sliced

1 large tomato, sliced

2 limes, cut into wedges, for serving

Working one at a time, place a pork cutlet between two sheets of plastic wrap. Use a heavy skillet or meat mallet to pound the pork to a ¼-inch thickness, being careful not to tear the meat. Season the cutlets on both sides with the adobo seasoning.

In a shallow bowl, beat the egg with 1 teaspoon water and the sazón. Place the bread crumbs in a second shallow bowl. Dip the cutlets into the egg mixture, letting the excess drip off, then dip them in the bread crumbs. Place the cutlets on a work surface and press lightly with the flat side of a heavy knife to help the bread crumbs adhere. Generously spray both sides with oil.

Preheat the air fryer to 400°F.

Working in batches, place the cutlets in the air fryer basket. Cook for 6 to 7 minutes, flipping halfway, until golden brown and the center is no longer pink. (For a toaster oven–style air fryer, the temperature remains the same; cook for 6 minutes.)

Divide the cutlets among 4 plates and serve with the avocado, tomato, and lime wedges. Serve immediately.

PER SERVING: **2 cutlets + one-quarter of the avocado and tomato** · CALORIES **395** · FAT **18.5 g** · SATURATED FAT **5 g** · CHOLESTEROL **140 mg** · CARBOHYDRATE **16 g** · FIBER **4.5 g** · PROTEIN **42 g** · SUGARS **3 g** · SODIUM **674 mg**

Q
GF
K

Apple-Stuffed Pork Chops

Pork and apples are a classic combination, so naturally, an apple-stuffed pork chop makes perfect sense—especially apples that have been sautéed with onions, celery, cinnamon, and nutmeg. I prefer bone-in pork chops as I think they're juicier, but if you like boneless, you can use them instead. Sautéed cabbage is the perfect side to make this a meal.

PORK

4 (6½ ounces each) bone-in, center-cut loin pork chops, trimmed

1 teaspoon kosher salt

½ teaspoon dried sage

½ teaspoon garlic powder

¼ teaspoon ground cinnamon

¼ teaspoon ground nutmeg

¼ teaspoon sweet paprika

⅛ teaspoon freshly ground black pepper

2 teaspoons Dijon mustard

2 teaspoons pure maple syrup

APPLE STUFFING

½ tablespoon unsalted butter

1 large sweet apple (Honeycrisp or Gala), peeled and thinly sliced

½ medium onion, chopped

¼ cup chopped celery

½ teaspoon kosher salt

½ teaspoon dried sage

½ teaspoon garlic powder

¼ teaspoon ground cinnamon

¼ teaspoon ground nutmeg

For the pork: Working with one chop at a time, place the pork between two sheets of plastic wrap. Use a heavy skillet or meat mallet to pound the pork to a ¾-inch thickness, being careful not to tear the meat. Cut a pocket in each chop horizontally, making sure not to cut all the way through.

In a small bowl, combine the salt, sage, garlic powder, cinnamon, nutmeg, paprika, and pepper. Season the inside and outside of each pork chop with the spice mix.

In a small bowl, mix together the mustard and maple syrup.

For the apple stuffing: In a large skillet, melt the butter over medium heat. Add the apple, onion, celery, salt, sage, garlic powder, cinnamon, and nutmeg. Cover and cook, stirring occasionally, until the apple and vegetables are softened, about 15 minutes. Dividing evenly, stuff the apple mixture (about ¼ cup each) into the pork chops.

Preheat the air fryer to 400°F.

Working in batches, place the stuffed pork chops in the air fryer basket. Cook for 3 minutes. Flip the chops and brush the tops with the mustard-maple mixture. Continue cooking for 3 to 4 minutes, until just cooked through. (For a toaster oven–style air fryer, cook at 375°F for 3 minutes, then for 2 to 3 minutes.) Carefully remove the chops with tongs to a platter. Tent with foil and let rest for 5 minutes (the meat will continue cooking). Serve warm.

PER SERVING: 1 chop • CALORIES 300 • FAT 9 g • SATURATED FAT 3 g • CHOLESTEROL 131 mg • CARBOHYDRATE 12 g • FIBER 2 g • PROTEIN 41 g • SUGARS 8 g • SODIUM 609 mg

Q
GF
DF
K

Five-Spice Glazed Lamb Chops

The combination of Chinese five-spice powder, honey, and brown sugar reminds me of char siu (Chinese BBQ pork), although it's much leaner when you use lamb chops as I do here. The dish needs a few hours to marinate, but once that's done, this dish comes together super fast in the air fryer, which creates perfectly juicy, flavorful chops. I leave the crushed red pepper flakes off a few chops for Madison and she loves them. To complete the meal, serve with brown rice and cucumber wedges.

8 (3½-ounce) bone-in lamb loin chops, trimmed

3 garlic cloves, crushed

¼ cup soy sauce* or tamari

¼ teaspoon Chinese five-spice powder

3 tablespoons honey

½ tablespoon light brown sugar

¼ teaspoon crushed red pepper flakes

Scallions, sliced into long, thin strips

*Read the label to be sure this product is gluten-free.

Place the lamb chops in a large bowl and season with the garlic, soy sauce, five-spice, and honey, tossing to coat well. Cover with plastic wrap and marinate in the refrigerator for at least 2 hours, or as long as overnight.

Preheat the air fryer to 400°F.

Working in batches, arrange a single layer of chops (reserve the marinade) in the air fryer basket and cook for 5 minutes. Flip the chops, brush the tops with the marinade, and sprinkle with the brown sugar and pepper flakes. Continue cooking until the top is browned and caramelized, 4 to 5 minutes for medium to medium-rare doneness; for well done, cook an additional 1 to 2 minutes. (For a toaster oven–style air fryer, the temperature and timing remain the same.) Top with the scallions and serve.

PER SERVING: 2 chops · CALORIES 308 · FAT 13.5 g · SATURATED FAT 5.5 g · CHOLESTEROL 132 mg · CARBOHYDRATE 7 g · FIBER 0.5 g · PROTEIN 40 g · SUGARS 6 g · SODIUM 406 mg

SEAFOOD

Q
GF
DF

Crispy Coconut Shrimp with Sweet Chili Mayo

Tommy claims these are the best coconut shrimp he's ever eaten, including from any restaurant! Making coconut shrimp in the air fryer gets the coating crisp and golden in just minutes—without soaking up a lot of oil as if you were to pan-fry them. The sweet and spicy mayo is the perfect complement for dipping, but the shrimp are perfectly delicious on their own, too. This dish makes a great appetizer, or you can serve the shrimp over a bed of greens and turn it into a salad.

SWEET CHILI MAYO

3 tablespoons mayonnaise

3 tablespoons Thai sweet chili sauce

1 tablespoon Sriracha sauce

SHRIMP

2/3 cup sweetened shredded coconut

2/3 cup panko bread crumbs, regular or gluten-free

Kosher salt

2 tablespoons all-purpose or gluten-free flour

2 large eggs

24 extra-jumbo shrimp (about 1 pound), peeled and deveined

Olive oil spray

For the sweet chili mayo: In a medium bowl, combine the mayonnaise, Thai sweet chili sauce, and Sriracha and mix well.

For the shrimp: In a medium bowl, combine the coconut, panko, and 1/4 teaspoon salt. Place the flour in a shallow bowl. Whisk the eggs in another shallow bowl.

Season the shrimp with 1/8 teaspoon salt. Dip the shrimp in the flour, shaking off any excess, then into the egg. Coat in the coconut-panko mixture, gently pressing to adhere, then transfer to a large plate. Spray both sides of the shrimp with oil.

Preheat the air fryer to 360°F.

Working in batches, arrange a single layer of the shrimp in the air fryer basket. Cook for about 8 minutes, flipping halfway, until the crust is golden brown and the shrimp are cooked through. (For a toaster oven–style air fryer, cook at 300°F; the timing remains the same.) Serve with the sweet chili mayo for dipping.

PER SERVING: **6 shrimp + 1 1/2 tablespoons sauce** · CALORIES **355** · FAT **16 g** · SATURATED FAT **6.5 g** · CHOLESTEROL **232 mg** · CARBOHYDRATE **25 g** · FIBER **1 g** · PROTEIN **25 g** · SUGARS **13 g** · SODIUM **750 mg**

Shrimp Empanadas

Empanadas bring me back to when I was kid and spent my summers in Puerto Rico. I ate empanadas (also known as *pastelillos)* from street vendors every chance I could. My favorites were the ones filled with lobster, shrimp, or pizza toppings. You can fill empanadas with just about anything you can dream up, from leftover taco meat or Buffalo chicken to pie filling for a sweet version. I stuff these empanadas with shrimp and they couldn't be easier to make because there is no need to precook the shrimp filling—it cooks right in the empanada dough. I make them in the air fryer with Goya empanada discs (the kind sold for baking), so they turn out golden and crisp in less than 10 minutes with no need for all that oil used to deep-fry.

½ pound peeled and deveined raw shrimp, chopped

¼ cup chopped red onion

1 scallion, chopped

2 garlic cloves, minced

2 tablespoons minced red bell pepper

2 tablespoons chopped fresh cilantro

½ tablespoon fresh lime juice

¼ teaspoon sweet paprika

⅛ teaspoon kosher salt

⅛ teaspoon crushed red pepper flakes (optional)

1 large egg, beaten

10 frozen Goya Empanada Discos (for baking), thawed

Cooking spray

In a medium bowl, combine the shrimp, red onion, scallion, garlic, bell pepper, cilantro, lime juice, paprika, salt, and pepper flakes (if using).

In a small bowl, beat the egg with 1 teaspoon water until smooth.

Place an empanada disc on a work surface and put 2 tablespoons of the shrimp mixture in the center. Brush the outer edges of the disc with the egg wash. Fold the disc over and gently press the edges to seal. Use a fork and press around the edges to crimp and seal completely. Brush the tops of the empanadas with the egg wash.

Preheat the air fryer to 380°F.

Spray the bottom of the air fryer basket with cooking spray to prevent sticking. Working in batches, arrange a single layer of the empanadas in the air fryer basket and cook for about 8 minutes, flipping halfway, until golden brown and crispy. (For a toaster oven–style air fryer, cook at 300°F for about 10 minutes.) Serve hot.

skinny scoop If you can't find the Goya discs for baking, the ones sold for frying will also work.

PER SERVING: **2 empanadas** · CALORIES **262** · FAT **11 g** · SATURATED FAT **6.5 g** · CHOLESTEROL **91 mg** · CARBOHYDRATE **26 g** · FIBER **1.5 g** · PROTEIN **13 g** · SUGARS **1 g** · SODIUM **482 mg**

Q
GF
DF
K

Lemony Shrimp and Zucchini with Mint

Fried dishes aren't the only foods you can make in an air fryer—in fact, anything you would typically roast in an oven can also be made in this ingenious kitchen tool. Here, I combined shrimp, zucchini, and fresh herbs for a simple dish that is ready in under 20 minutes, making it a weeknight win! A simple side dish of orzo or rice pilaf would be the perfect complement.

1¼ pounds peeled and deveined extra-large raw shrimp

2 medium zucchini (about 8 ounces each), halved lengthwise and cut into ½-inch-thick slices

1½ tablespoons olive oil

½ teaspoon garlic salt

1½ teaspoons dried oregano

⅛ teaspoon crushed red pepper flakes (optional)

Juice of ½ lemon

1 tablespoon chopped fresh mint

1 tablespoon chopped fresh dill

Preheat the air fryer to 350°F.

In a large bowl, combine the shrimp, zucchini, oil, garlic salt, oregano, and pepper flakes (if using) and toss to coat.

Working in batches, arrange a single layer of the shrimp and zucchini in the air fryer basket. Cook, shaking the basket halfway, until the zucchini is golden and the shrimp are cooked through, 7 to 8 minutes. (For a toaster oven–style air fryer, the temperature and timing remain the same.) Transfer to a serving dish and tent with foil while you cook the remaining shrimp and zucchini.

Top with the lemon juice, mint, and dill and serve.

PER SERVING: 1¼ cups • CALORIES 194 • FAT 6 g • SATURATED FAT 1 g • CHOLESTEROL 169 mg • CARBOHYDRATE 6 g • FIBER 1.5 g • PROTEIN 27 g • SUGARS 3 g • SODIUM 481 mg

Q
GF
DF

Tortilla Shrimp Tacos
with Cilantro-Lime Slaw

In my house, taco night happens at least once a week! It never gets boring because we switch it up every time, like with these tortilla-crusted shrimp tacos. They're ridiculously quick to whip up and so darn delicious you might want to make them on repeat. The crushed corn tortilla chips make the perfect crispy crust for the shrimp.

SPICY MAYO

3 tablespoons mayonnaise

1 tablespoon Louisiana-style
  hot pepper sauce

CILANTRO-LIME SLAW

2 cups shredded green
  cabbage

½ small red onion, thinly
  sliced

1 small jalapeño, thinly sliced

2 tablespoons chopped fresh
  cilantro

Juice of 1 lime

¼ teaspoon kosher salt

SHRIMP

1 large egg, beaten

1 cup crushed tortilla chips
  (4 ounces)

24 jumbo shrimp (about
  1 pound), peeled and
  deveined

⅛ teaspoon kosher salt

Olive oil spray

8 corn tortillas, for serving

For the spicy mayo: In a small bowl, mix together the mayonnaise and hot pepper sauce.

For the cilantro-lime slaw: In a large bowl, toss together the cabbage, onion, jalapeño, cilantro, lime juice, and salt to combine. Cover and refrigerate to chill.

For the shrimp: Place the egg in a shallow bowl and the crushed tortilla chips in another. Season the shrimp with the salt. Dip the shrimp in the egg, then in the crumbs, pressing gently to adhere. Place on a work surface and spray both sides with oil.

Preheat the air fryer to 360°F.

Working in batches, arrange a single layer of the shrimp in the air fryer basket. Cook for 6 minutes, flipping halfway, until golden and cooked through in the center. (For a toaster oven–style air fryer, cook at 350°F for 5 minutes.)

To serve, place 2 tortillas on each plate and top each with 3 shrimp. Top each taco with ¼ cup slaw, then drizzle with spicy mayo.

skinny scoop To crush the tortilla chips, place them in a gallon-size zip-top bag and use a rolling pin to roll them until finely crushed.

PER SERVING: **2 tacos** · CALORIES **440** · FAT **17 g** · SATURATED FAT **2.5 g** · CHOLESTEROL **186 mg** · CARBOHYDRATE **44 g** · FIBER **6 g** · PROTEIN **27 g** · SUGARS **3 g** · SODIUM **590 mg**

Q
GF
DF

Crab Cake Sandwiches with Cajun Mayo

If you love crab cakes like I do (with lots of meat and very little bread crumb), you will just flip for these! Served on soft potato buns with a delicious Cajun-spiced mayo, these sandwiches will take you right to your favorite summer seafood shack.

CRAB CAKES

½ cup panko bread crumbs, regular or gluten-free

1 large egg, beaten

1 large egg white

1 tablespoon mayonnaise

1 teaspoon Dijon mustard

¼ cup minced fresh parsley

1 tablespoon fresh lemon juice

½ teaspoon Old Bay seasoning

⅛ teaspoon sweet paprika

⅛ teaspoon kosher salt

Freshly ground black pepper

10 ounces lump crabmeat

Olive oil spray

CAJUN MAYO

¼ cup mayonnaise

1 tablespoon minced dill pickle

1 teaspoon fresh lemon juice

¾ teaspoon Cajun seasoning*

FOR SERVING

4 Boston lettuce leaves

4 whole wheat potato buns or gluten-free buns

For the crab cakes: In a large bowl, combine the panko, whole egg, egg white, mayonnaise, mustard, parsley, lemon juice, Old Bay, paprika, salt, and pepper to taste and mix well. Fold in the crabmeat, being careful not to overmix. Gently shape into 4 round patties, about ½ cup each, ¾ inch thick. Spray both sides with oil.

Preheat the air fryer to 370°F.

Working in batches, place the crab cakes in the air fryer basket. Cook about 10 minutes, flipping halfway, until the edges are golden. (For a toaster oven–style air fryer, cook at 350°F; the timing remains the same.)

Meanwhile, for the Cajun mayo: In a small bowl, combine the mayonnaise, pickle, lemon juice, and Cajun seasoning.

To serve: Place a lettuce leaf on each bun bottom and top with a crab cake and a generous tablespoon of Cajun mayonnaise. Add the bun top and serve.

skinny scoop To enjoy this gluten-free, use gluten-free buns or skip the bun altogether and serve the crab cake over a bed of butter lettuce.

*Read the label to be sure this product is gluten-free.

PER SERVING: **1 sandwich** · CALORIES **354** · FAT **18.5 g** · SATURATED FAT **2.5 g** · CHOLESTEROL **123 mg** · CARBOHYDRATE **25 g** · FIBER **3.5 g** · PROTEIN **25 g** · SUGARS **5 g** · SODIUM **914 mg**

Q
GF
DF
K

Blackened Salmon
with Cucumber-Avocado Salsa

From start to finish, this dinner takes under 20 minutes—now that's a recipe for success! I prefer to make my own blackening spice mix so I can control the heat. This one is mildly spicy, and it pairs perfectly with the cooling cucumber-avocado salsa. If you like it hot, just increase the cayenne pepper!

SALMON

1 tablespoon sweet paprika

½ teaspoon cayenne pepper

1 teaspoon garlic powder

1 teaspoon dried oregano

1 teaspoon dried thyme

¾ teaspoon kosher salt

⅛ teaspoon freshly ground black pepper

Olive oil spray

4 (6 ounces each) wild salmon fillets

CUCUMBER-AVOCADO SALSA

2 tablespoons chopped red onion

1½ tablespoons fresh lemon juice

1 teaspoon extra-virgin olive oil

¼ teaspoon plus ⅛ teaspoon kosher salt

Freshly ground black pepper

4 Persian (mini) cucumbers, diced

6 ounces Hass avocado (from 1 large), diced

For the salmon: In a small bowl, combine the paprika, cayenne, garlic powder, oregano, thyme, salt, and black pepper. Spray both sides of the fish with oil and rub all over. Coat the fish all over with the spices.

For the cucumber-avocado salsa: In a medium bowl, combine the red onion, lemon juice, olive oil, salt, and pepper to taste. Let stand for 5 minutes, then add the cucumbers and avocado.

Preheat the air fryer to 400°F.

Working in batches, arrange the salmon fillets skin side down in the air fryer basket. Cook until the fish flakes easily with a fork, 5 to 7 minutes, depending on the thickness of the fish. (For a toaster oven–style air fryer, the temperature and timing remain the same.) Serve topped with the salsa.

PER SERVING: 1 fish fillet + ¾ cup salsa · CALORIES 340 · FAT 18.5 g · SATURATED FAT 3 g · CHOLESTEROL 94 mg · CARBOHYDRATE 8 g · FIBER 4 g · PROTEIN 35 g · SUGARS 2 g · SODIUM 396 mg

Q
GF
DF
K

Roasted Fish with Lemon-Almond Crumbs

This simple almond topping—prepared with chopped almonds, lemon zest, and scallion—has plenty of crunch, flavor, and texture, making it a great healthier alternative for "breaded" fish. It's perfect if you're on a low-carb diet (or not!). Plus, the almonds contain nutrients and healthy fats that will keep you feeling satisfied. This recipe works with any white fish, but just keep in mind that the cook time will vary slightly depending on the thickness of the fish.

½ cup raw whole almonds

1 scallion, finely chopped

Grated zest and juice of 1 lemon

½ tablespoon extra-virgin olive oil

¾ teaspoon kosher salt

Freshly ground black pepper

4 (6 ounces each) skinless fish fillets, such as halibut, black cod, or sea bass

Olive oil spray

1 teaspoon Dijon mustard

In a food processor, pulse the almonds to coarsely chop. Transfer to a small bowl and add the scallion, lemon zest, and olive oil. Season with ¼ teaspoon of the salt and pepper to taste and mix to combine.

Spray the top of the fish with oil and squeeze the lemon juice over the fish. Season with the remaining ½ teaspoon salt and pepper to taste. Spread the mustard on top of the fish. Dividing evenly, press the almond mixture onto the top of the fillets to adhere.

Preheat the air fryer to 375°F.

Working in batches, place the fillets in the air fryer basket in a single layer. Cook until the crumbs start to brown and the fish is cooked through, 7 to 8 minutes, or longer depending on the thickness of the fillet. (For a toaster oven–style air fryer, cook at 350°F for about 7 minutes.) Serve immediately.

PER SERVING: 1 fillet · CALORIES 282 · FAT 13 g · SATURATED FAT 1.5 g · CHOLESTEROL 83 mg · CARBOHYDRATE 6 g · FIBER 2.5 g · PROTEIN 36 g · SUGARS 1 g · SODIUM 359 mg

Q
GF

Fish Croquettes with Lemon-Dill Aioli

I grew up eating (and loving!) potato croquettes. My mom would make them with leftover chicken or turkey, but fish croquettes were always one of my favorites. The croquettes work with any kind of flaky, white fish (I tested them with cod). Rather than using potatoes, Mom's speedy secret was boxed mashed potatoes (they actually hold together better, too). This simple lemon-dill aioli really makes it spectacular! Serve with a cucumber salad to turn it into a meal.

CROQUETTES

3 large eggs

12 ounces raw cod fillet, flaked apart with two forks

¼ cup 1% milk

½ cup boxed instant mashed potatoes (such as Idahoan)

2 teaspoons olive oil

⅓ cup chopped fresh dill

1 shallot, minced

1 large garlic clove, minced

¾ cup plus 2 tablespoons bread crumbs, regular or gluten-free

1 teaspoon fresh lemon juice

1 teaspoon kosher salt

½ teaspoon dried thyme

¼ teaspoon freshly ground black pepper

Olive oil spray

LEMON-DILL AIOLI

5 tablespoons mayonnaise

Juice of ½ lemon

1 tablespoon chopped fresh dill

For the croquettes: In a medium bowl, lightly beat 2 of the eggs. Add the fish, milk, instant mashed potatoes, olive oil, dill, shallot, garlic, 2 tablespoons of the bread crumbs, the lemon juice, salt, thyme, and pepper. Mix to thoroughly combine. Place in the refrigerator for 30 minutes.

For the lemon-dill aioli: In a small bowl, combine the mayonnaise, lemon juice, and dill.

Measure out about 3½ tablespoons of the fish mixture and gently roll in your hands to form a log about 3 inches long. Repeat to make a total of 12 logs.

Beat the remaining egg in a small bowl. Place the remaining ¾ cup bread crumbs in a separate bowl. Dip the croquettes in the egg, then coat in the bread crumbs, gently pressing to adhere. Place on a work surface and spray both sides with oil.

Preheat the air fryer to 350°F.

Working in batches, arrange a single layer of the croquettes in the air fryer basket. Cook for about 10 minutes, flipping halfway, until golden. (For a toaster oven–style air fryer, the temperature remains the same; cook for 8 minutes.) Serve with the aioli for dipping.

PER SERVING: **3 croquettes + 1½ tablespoons sauce** • CALORIES **461** • FAT **21.5 g** • SATURATED FAT **4 g** • CHOLESTEROL **183 mg** • CARBOHYDRATE **41 g** • FIBER **3.5 g** • PROTEIN **26 g** • SUGARS **5 g** • SODIUM **652 mg**

Salmon Burgers
with Lemon-Caper Rémoulade

Finely grinding part of the salmon to use as a binder allows you to use less panko, so the burgers come out moist every time. If you want to go bun-less, swap it out and serve the burger over a bed of lettuce.

LEMON-CAPER RÉMOULADE

½ cup mayonnaise

2 tablespoons drained capers, minced

2 tablespoons chopped fresh parsley

2 teaspoons fresh lemon juice

SALMON PATTIES

1 pound wild salmon fillet, skinned and pin bones removed

6 tablespoons panko bread crumbs, regular or gluten-free

¼ cup minced red onion plus ¼ cup slivered for assembly

1 garlic clove, minced

1 large egg, lightly beaten

1 tablespoon Dijon mustard

1 teaspoon fresh lemon juice

1 tablespoon chopped fresh parsley

½ teaspoon kosher salt

FOR SERVING

5 whole wheat potato buns or gluten-free buns

10 butter lettuce leaves

For the lemon-caper rémoulade: In a small bowl, combine the mayonnaise, capers, parsley, and lemon juice and mix well.

For the salmon patties: Cut off a 4-ounce piece of the salmon and transfer to a food processor. Pulse until it becomes pasty. (This will help hold the burgers together.) With a sharp knife, chop the remaining salmon into small cubes.

In a medium bowl, combine the chopped and processed salmon with the panko, minced red onion, garlic, egg, mustard, lemon juice, parsley, and salt. Toss gently to combine. Form the mixture into 5 patties about ¾ inch thick. Refrigerate for at least 30 minutes (this helps the patties hold together better when cooking).

Preheat the air fryer to 400°F.

Working in batches, place the patties in the air fryer basket. Cook for about 12 minutes, gently flipping halfway, until golden and cooked through. (For a toaster oven–style air fryer, the temperature and timing remain the same.)

To serve: Transfer each patty to a bun. Top each with 2 lettuce leaves, 2 tablespoons of the rémoulade, and the slivered red onions.

skinny scoop When purchasing salmon, seek out a reputable fishmonger. I always buy wild varieties and look for salmon that was flash frozen when caught and hasn't been sitting too long once thawed.

PER SERVING: **1 burger** · CALORIES **436** · FAT **26.5 g** · SATURATED FAT **4 g** · CHOLESTEROL **96 mg** · CARBOHYDRATE **24 g** · FIBER **4 g** · PROTEIN **28 g** · SUGARS **5 g** · SODIUM **616 mg**

VEGETABLE MAINS & SIDES

Q
V
GF
K

Tomato, Spinach, and Feta Stuffed Portobellos

Portobellos are meaty and juicy, the perfect blank slate for stuffing with anything you can imagine! Here, this winning combination of fresh tomatoes, spinach, herbs, and cheese is simply delicious, and so easy to make because you don't have to precook anything—just stuff them and cook everything at the same time. Enjoy them as a meatless main with salad or quinoa, or serve as a side dish to chicken or fish.

4 large portobello mushroom caps (about 3 ounces each)

Olive oil spray

Kosher salt

2 medium plum tomatoes, chopped

1 cup baby spinach, roughly chopped

¾ cup crumbled feta cheese

1 shallot, chopped

1 large garlic clove, minced

¼ cup chopped fresh basil

2 tablespoons panko bread crumbs, regular or gluten-free

1 tablespoon chopped fresh oregano

1 tablespoon freshly grated Parmesan cheese

⅛ teaspoon freshly ground black pepper

1 tablespoon olive oil

Balsamic glaze (optional), for drizzling

Use a small metal spoon to carefully scrape the black gills out of each mushroom cap. Spray both sides of the mushrooms with olive oil and season with a pinch of salt.

In a medium bowl, combine the tomatoes, spinach, feta, shallot, garlic, basil, panko, oregano, Parmesan, ¼ teaspoon salt, pepper, and olive oil and mix well. Carefully fill the inside of each mushroom cap with the mixture.

Preheat the air fryer to 370°F.

Working in batches, arrange a single layer of the stuffed mushrooms in the air fryer basket. Cook for 10 to 12 minutes, until the mushrooms are tender and the top is golden. (For a toaster oven–style air fryer, place the basket in the lower rack position and cook at 375°F for about 10 minutes.) Use a flexible spatula to carefully remove the mushrooms from the basket and transfer to a serving dish. Drizzle the balsamic glaze (if using) over the mushrooms and serve.

skinny scoop Portobello mushroom caps should be kept dry and refrigerated until ready to use; they will keep for up to a week. Look for mushrooms with deep unbroken sides to keep the cheese from oozing out.

PER SERVING: **1 stuffed cap** · CALORIES **160** · FAT **10 g** · SATURATED FAT **5 g** · CHOLESTEROL **26 mg** · CARBOHYDRATE **11 g** · FIBER **3 g** · PROTEIN **8 g** · SUGARS **6 g** · SODIUM **498 mg**

Sesame-Crusted Teriyaki Tofu "Steaks"

If you've never tried tofu before and are unsure whether you'll like it or not, this dish might be the one to win you over! It's incredibly simple to make, the crunchy sesame crust gives tofu a major textural boost, and the teriyaki marinade is so good. I swear this dish could convert even the most devout tofu-hater. I tested it out on my family, and we all agreed this recipe is a keeper! Serve with brown rice or cauliflower rice, and some edamame or stir-fried veggies to make this a meal.

TOFU

7 ounces extra-firm tofu (about ½ block), drained and cut into 4 (½-inch-thick) slices

2 tablespoons reduced-sodium soy sauce* or tamari

1 teaspoon toasted sesame oil

1 teaspoon unseasoned rice vinegar

1 teaspoon light brown sugar

1 garlic clove, grated

½ teaspoon grated fresh ginger

⅓ cup white and black sesame seeds

1 large egg

Olive oil spray

SRIRACHA MAYO

4 teaspoons mayonnaise

1 teaspoon Sriracha sauce

1 scallion, chopped, for garnish (optional)

*Read the label to be sure this product is gluten-free.

For the tofu: Place the tofu slices on a kitchen towel or paper towels. Place another towel on top and lightly press to remove most of the water from the tofu. Transfer to a shallow bowl or baking dish big enough for the tofu to lie in a single layer.

In a small bowl, whisk together the soy sauce, sesame oil, vinegar, brown sugar, garlic, and ginger. Drizzle half of the marinade over the tofu, then gently flip and drizzle the rest on the other side. Marinate in the refrigerator for at least 1 hour, or up to overnight.

Place the sesame seeds on a small plate or pie dish. In another small dish or bowl, beat the egg. Remove each tofu slice from the marinade, allowing the excess to drip off, then dip in the egg. Using a fork, dip in the sesame seeds, coating each side. Transfer to a work surface. Spray one side with olive oil, then gently flip and spray the other side. (Discard the excess marinade.)

Preheat the air fryer to 400°F.

Working in batches, arrange a single layer of the tofu in the air fryer basket. Cook for about 10 minutes, flipping halfway, until toasted and crisp. (For a toaster oven–style air fryer, cook at 350°F for about 8 minutes.)

Meanwhile, for the Sriracha mayo: In a small bowl, combine the mayonnaise and Sriracha.

To serve, top each tofu "steak" with the Sriracha mayo and some scallion (if using).

PER SERVING: 2 "steaks" + 2½ teaspoons sauce · CALORIES 321 · FAT 24.5 g · SATURATED FAT 4 g · CHOLESTEROL 50 mg · CARBOHYDRATE 14 g · FIBER 4.5 g · PROTEIN 14 g · SUGARS 4 g · SODIUM 716 mg

Q
V
GF

Buffalo Cauliflower Nuggets

Cauliflower can be turned into just about anything, from rice or faux mashed potatoes to pizza crust—you name it! But one of my all-time favorite ways to get my cauliflower-averse family members to eat this cruciferous veggie is by lightly battering it in egg, flouring it, then air-frying and smothering it in hot sauce. You can make these spicy nuggets for game day or any day of the week—just serve with blue cheese dip to tame the heat!

3 large eggs, beaten

1/2 cup all-purpose or gluten-free flour

28 bite-size (about 1 1/2-inch) cauliflower florets (16 ounces)

Olive oil spray

6 tablespoons Frank's RedHot sauce

1 tablespoon unsalted butter, melted

Blue cheese dip, homemade (page 32) or store-bought (optional)

Carrot sticks and celery sticks, for serving (optional)

Preheat the air fryer to 380°F.

Place the eggs in a small bowl. Place the flour in a separate medium bowl. Dip the cauliflower into the egg, then into the flour to coat, shaking off the excess. Place on a work surface and spray both sides with oil.

Working in batches, arrange a single layer of the cauliflower in the air fryer basket. Cook for 7 to 8 minutes, flipping halfway, until golden and tender. When all the batches are done, return all the cauliflower to the air fryer and cook for 1 minute to heat through. (For a toaster oven–style air fryer, cook at 350°F; the ming remains the same.) Transfer to a large bowl and toss with the hot sauce and melted butter. If desired, serve with blue cheese dressing and vegetable sticks.

skinny scoop You can swap the flour for almond flour to make these low-carb and keto-friendly.

PER SERVING: **7 pieces** • CALORIES **143** • FAT **6.5 g** • SATURATED FAT **3 g** • CHOLESTEROL **147 mg** • CARBOHYDRATE **14 g** • FIBER **3 g** • PROTEIN **8 g** • SUGARS **3 g** • SODIUM **943 mg**

Q
V
GF

Mexican Street Corn

When I go to Queens in New York City, I can never resist buying Mexican-style grilled corn on the cob from the street vendors. Topped with generous amounts of mayo, Cotija cheese, cilantro, ancho powder, and lime, it's so delicious! Turns out, sweet summer corn cooks up tender and crisp in the air fryer, so this is a snap to make at home. And since it's really messy to hold the traditional version with your hands, I cut the corn off the cob for easy eating.

4 medium ears corn, husked

Olive oil spray

2 tablespoons mayonnaise

1 tablespoon fresh lime juice

½ teaspoon ancho chile powder

¼ teaspoon kosher salt

2 ounces crumbled Cotija or feta cheese

2 tablespoons chopped fresh cilantro

Preheat the air fryer to 375°F.

Spritz the corn with olive oil. Working in batches, arrange the ears of corn in the air fryer basket in a single layer. Cook for about 7 minutes, flipping halfway, until the kernels are tender when pierced with a paring knife. (For a toaster oven–style air fryer, cook at 350°F for about 6 minutes.) When cool enough to handle, cut the corn kernels off the cob.

In a large bowl, mix together mayonnaise, lime juice, ancho powder, and salt. Add the corn kernels and mix to combine. Transfer to a serving dish and top with the Cotija and cilantro. Serve immediately.

PER SERVING: ¾ cup · CALORIES 181 · FAT 10.5 g · SATURATED FAT 3.5 g · CHOLESTEROL 18 mg · CARBOHYDRATE 19 g · FIBER 3 g · PROTEIN 7 g · SUGARS 3 g · SODIUM 329 mg

Sugar and Spice Acorn Squash

Perfectly sweet and easy to make, this autumn treat is a great side dish to serve with pork chops or pork loin. What I love most about making this recipe is the house smelling like fall as the cinnamon-and-nutmeg-spiced squash roasts. Look for an acorn squash that is firm and heavy for its size.

1 teaspoon coconut oil (I use virgin)

1 medium acorn squash, halved crosswise and seeded

1 teaspoon light brown sugar

Few dashes of ground nutmeg

Few dashes of ground cinnamon

Rub the coconut oil on the cut sides of the squash. Sprinkle with the brown sugar, nutmeg, and cinnamon.

Preheat the air fryer to 325°F.

Place the squash halves, cut sides up, in the air fryer basket. Cook for 15 minutes, until soft in the center when pierced with a paring knife. (For a toaster oven–style air fryer, cook at 300°F; the timing remains the same.) Serve immediately.

skinny scoop Microwave the squash on high for 2 to 3 minutes to make it easier to cut.

PER SERVING: 1 squash half · CALORIES 114 · FAT 2.5 g · SATURATED FAT 2 g · CHOLESTEROL 0 mg · CARBOHYDRATE 25 g · FIBER 3 g · PROTEIN 2 g · SUGARS 2 g · SODIUM 7 mg

Brussels Sprouts with Bacon

Brussels sprouts—love them or hate them? For some, those two words are cringe-worthy, but it doesn't have to be that way! Cooking Brussels sprouts until fork-tender with a crispy, browned surface is a total game changer. Bacon and Brussels sprouts are a classic combination: The rich, smoky flavors from the crispy bacon complement the slight bitterness of the sprouts.

3 slices center-cut bacon, halved

1 pound Brussels sprouts, trimmed and halved

1½ tablespoons extra-virgin olive oil

¼ teaspoon kosher salt

¼ teaspoon dried thyme

Preheat the air fryer to 350°F.

Arrange the bacon in a single layer in the air fryer basket. Cook for about 10 minutes, until crisp. Transfer the bacon to a plate lined with paper towels to drain, then roughly chop. (For a toaster oven–style air fryer, the temperature remains the same; cook for about 8 minutes.)

In a large bowl, toss the Brussels sprouts with the oil. Sprinkle with the salt and thyme and toss well to coat.

Working in batches, arrange a single layer of the Brussels sprouts in the air fryer basket. Cook for about 13 minutes, shaking halfway, until golden brown and tender. (For a toaster oven–style air fryer, the temperature remains the same; cook for about 10 minutes.) Transfer to a serving dish, top with the bacon, and serve.

skinny scoop When preparing Brussels sprouts, try to select a bunch with a consistent size. Larger ones may take a few minutes longer to cook, while smaller ones a few minutes less. Be sure to peel away any discolored outer leaves.

PER SERVING: 2/3 cup · CALORIES 116 · FAT 7 g · SATURATED FAT 1.5 g · CHOLESTEROL 2 mg · CARBOHYDRATE 10 g · FIBER 4.5 g · PROTEIN 6 g · SUGARS 2 g · SODIUM 189 mg

Q
V
GF
DF
K

Charred Sesame Green Beans

Say hello to my new favorite way to prepare green beans! I've never been a fan of steamed green beans, but these, cooked until crisp and charred (so easy to do in the air fryer), are anything but bland and boring! Plus, they're tossed in a spicy soy-sesame sauce that makes them addictively good. I can easily eat the whole batch in one sitting. This side dish would pair perfectly with salmon or tofu.

1 tablespoon reduced-sodium soy sauce* or tamari

½ tablespoon Sriracha sauce

4 teaspoons toasted sesame oil

12 ounces trimmed green beans

½ tablespoon toasted sesame seeds

*Read the label to be sure this product is gluten-free.

In a small bowl, combine the soy sauce, Sriracha, and 1 teaspoon of the sesame oil.

In a large bowl, combine the green beans with the remaining 3 teaspoons sesame oil and toss to coat.

Preheat the air fryer to 375°F.

Working in batches, arrange a single layer of the green beans in the air fryer basket. Cook for about 8 minutes, shaking the basket halfway, until charred and tender. (For a toaster oven–style air fryer, cook at 350°F for about 9 minutes.) Transfer to a serving dish. Toss with the sauce and sesame seeds and serve.

skinny scoop For an Italian-inspired variation, omit the sesame oil, soy sauce, and Sriracha, and instead, season the beans with olive oil and ¼ teaspoon each salt and garlic powder. Toss the cooked beans with shredded Parmesan cheese.

PER SERVING: ½ cup · CALORIES 77 · FAT 5 g · SATURATED FAT 1 g · CHOLESTEROL 0 mg · CARBOHYDRATE 7 g · FIBER 3 g · PROTEIN 2 g · SUGARS 2 g · SODIUM 169 mg

Q
GF
DF
K

Bacon-Wrapped Asparagus Bundles

I like to think of these as little bundles of joy! Small bunches of asparagus are seasoned with a bit of lemon zest, wrapped in bacon, and air-fried until crisp on the outside and juicy in the center. They make a perfect addition to chicken, steaks, or pork chops. Note that the cook time may vary slightly depending on the thickness of the spears.

20 asparagus spears (12 ounces), tough ends trimmed

Olive oil spray

½ teaspoon grated lemon zest

⅛ teaspoon kosher salt

Freshly ground black pepper

4 slices center-cut bacon

Place the asparagus on a small sheet pan and spritz with olive oil. Season with the lemon zest, salt, and pepper to taste, tossing to coat. Group the asparagus into 4 bundles of 5 spears and wrap the center of each bundle with a slice of bacon.

Preheat the air fryer to 400°F.

Working in batches, place the asparagus bundles in the air fryer basket. Cook until the bacon is browned and the asparagus is slightly charred on the edges, 8 to 10 minutes, depending on the thickness of the spears. (For a toaster oven-style air fryer, the temperature and timing remain the same.) Serve immediately.

skinny scoop To keep asparagus fresh and hydrated until I'm ready to cook, I trim off the ends and keep them upright in a jar of water in the refrigerator, much as you would with fresh-cut flowers.

PER SERVING: **1 bundle** · CALORIES **47** · FAT **2.5 g** · SATURATED FAT **1 g** · CHOLESTEROL **3 mg** · CARBOHYDRATE **3 g** · FIBER **2 g** · PROTEIN **4 g** · SUGARS **2 g** · SODIUM **157 mg**

Q
V
GF
DF

French Fries

Crispy, delicious fries without all the grease? Sign me up! While many air fryer french fry recipes call for soaking the potatoes in water first, I find they turn out perfectly crisp without the extra step and time. The tricks: cutting the potatoes into even ¼-inch-thick fries, not overcrowding the basket, and flipping them halfway through. You can season them any way you desire. I love this basic seasoning mix, but they are also great topped with grated Parmesan cheese.

2 (6-ounce) Yukon Gold or russet potatoes, washed and dried

2 teaspoons olive oil

¼ teaspoon kosher salt

¼ teaspoon garlic powder

Freshly ground black pepper

Cut the potatoes lengthwise into ¼-inch-thick slices, then cut each slice into ¼-inch-thick fries.

In a medium bowl, toss the potatoes with the oil. Season with the salt, garlic powder, and pepper to taste, tossing to coat.

Preheat the air fryer to 380°F.

Working in batches, arrange a single layer (no overlapping) of the potatoes in the air fryer basket. Cook for 12 to 15 minutes, flipping halfway, until the potatoes are golden and crisp. (For a toaster oven–style air fryer, cook at 350°F; the timing remains the same.) Serve immediately.

skinny scoop: A mandoline slicer is very helpful here in producing uniformly thin slices. Also note that if your fries are cut thicker than this, they will take longer to cook.

PER SERVING: ½ batch • CALORIES 175 • FAT 4.5 g • SATURATED FAT 0.5 g • CHOLESTEROL 0 mg • CARBOHYDRATE 31 g • FIBER 2 g • PROTEIN 4 g • SUGARS 1 g • SODIUM 149 mg

Q
V
GF

Cheddar Broccoli Gratin

This easy side dish is pure broccoli bliss, featuring tender broccoli florets with caramelized edges and a crispy-cheesy topping. You know what else is awesome? With the air fryer, the time it takes to whip this dish up is minimal—I'm talking 15 minutes tops. Simply toss everything together, pour into a baking dish, and press start. Who's in?

Olive oil spray

½ tablespoon olive oil

1 tablespoon all-purpose or gluten-free flour

⅓ cup fat-free milk

½ teaspoon ground sage

¼ teaspoon kosher salt

⅛ teaspoon freshly ground black pepper

2 cups (5 ounces) broccoli florets, roughly chopped

6 tablespoons (1½ ounces) shredded extra-sharp cheddar cheese

2 tablespoons panko bread crumbs, regular or gluten-free

1 tablespoon freshly grated Parmesan cheese

Spray a 16-ounce round baking dish (about 7 inches) or a 7-inch cake pan with oil.

In a medium bowl, whisk together the olive oil, flour, milk, sage, salt, and pepper. Add the broccoli, cheddar, panko, and Parmesan and mix well. Transfer to the baking dish.

Preheat the air fryer to 330°F.

Place the baking dish in the air fryer basket. Cook for 12 to 14 minutes, until the broccoli is crisp-tender and the cheese is golden brown on top. (For a toaster oven–style air fryer, cook the gratin in a small rectangular baking dish at 300°F for 10 to 12 minutes.) Serve immediately.

PER SERVING: ¾ cup · CALORIES 193 · FAT 11.5 g · SATURATED FAT 5.5 g · CHOLESTEROL 25 mg · CARBOHYDRATE 13 g · FIBER 2 g · PROTEIN 10 g · SUGARS 4 g · SODIUM 359 mg

Crispy Onion Rings

Call me crazy, but I've always preferred onion rings over french fries, and I still do! I can honestly say these extra-crunchy, air-fried onion rings (breaded in cornflake crumbs and bread crumbs) are far better than any greasy, deep-fried versions out there.

1 medium Vidalia onion (about 9 ounces)

1½ cups (1½ ounces) cornflakes

½ cup seasoned bread crumbs

½ teaspoon sweet paprika

½ cup 1% buttermilk

1 large egg

¼ cup all-purpose flour

½ teaspoon kosher salt

Olive oil spray

Trim the ends off the onion, then quarter the onion crosswise (about ⅓-inch-thick slices) and separate into rings.

In a food processor, pulse the cornflakes until fine. Transfer to a medium bowl and stir in the bread crumbs and paprika. In another medium bowl, whisk together the buttermilk, egg, flour, and ½ teaspoon salt until combined.

Working in batches, dip the onion rings in the buttermilk batter, then into the cornflake mixture to coat. Set aside on a work surface and spray both sides with oil.

Preheat the air fryer to 340°F.

Working in batches, arrange a single layer of the onion rings in the air fryer basket. Cook for about 10 minutes, flipping halfway, until golden brown. (For a toaster oven–style air fryer, cook at 300°F; the timing remains the same.) Serve immediately.

PER SERVING: **about 5 rings** · CALORIES **132** · FAT **1.5 g** · SATURATED FAT **0.5 g** · CHOLESTEROL **31 mg** · CARBOHYDRATE **25 g** · FIBER **1.5 g** · PROTEIN **5 g** · SUGARS **6 g** · SODIUM **413 mg**

Perfectly Baked Potatoes with Yogurt and Chives

Restaurant-style baked potatoes come out perfectly cooked from the air fryer—fluffy on the inside and crispy, salted skin on the outside—and are ready in a fraction of the time it would take to make in the oven. This recipe is a blank slate: I simply top mine with some Greek yogurt and chives, but feel free to add your favorite toppings, such as broccoli and cheese, chili, or bacon.

4 (7-ounce) russet potatoes, washed and dried

Olive oil spray

½ teaspoon kosher salt

½ cup 2% Greek yogurt

¼ cup minced fresh chives

Freshly ground black pepper

Using a fork, pierce the potatoes all over. Spray each potato with a few spritzes of oil. Season the potatoes with ¼ teaspoon of the salt.

Preheat the air fryer to 400°F.

Place the potatoes in the air fryer basket. Cook for about 35 minutes, flipping halfway through, until a knife can easily be inserted into the center of each potato. (For a toaster oven-style air fryer, cook at 350°F; the timing remains the same.)

Split open the potatoes and serve topped with the yogurt, chives, the remaining ¼ teaspoon salt, and pepper to taste.

PER SERVING: 1 potato · CALORIES 162 · FAT 0.5 g · SATURATED FAT 0.5 mg · CHOLESTEROL 3 mg · CARBOHYDRATE 37 g · FIBER 2.5 g · PROTEIN 7 g · SUGARS 2 g · SODIUM 159 mg

Q
V
GF
DF

Crispy Sweet Potato Fries

Sweet potato fries cooked in the air fryer come out perfectly delicious, with just the right balance of crispy on the outside and creamy potato on the inside. Just be sure to try to cut the potatoes the same size. This way, all the fries finish at the same time, without pieces that are burnt, overcooked, or undercooked.

2 (6-ounce) sweet potatoes, peeled

2 teaspoons olive oil

1/2 teaspoon kosher salt

1/2 teaspoon garlic powder

1/4 teaspoon sweet paprika

Freshly ground black pepper

Cut the potatoes lengthwise into 1/4-inch-thick slices, then cut each slice into 1/4-inch-thick fries. Transfer to a large bowl and toss with the oil, salt, garlic powder, paprika, and pepper to taste.

Preheat the air fryer to 400°F.

Working in batches, arrange a single layer of the fries in the air fryer basket. Cook for about 8 minutes, flipping halfway, until golden brown and crisp on the outside. (For a toaster oven–style air fryer, cook at 350°F for 8 to 10 minutes.) Serve immediately.

skinny scoop: A mandoline slicer is very helpful here in producing uniformly thin slices. Also note that if your fries are cut thicker than this, they will take longer to cook.

PER SERVING: 1/2 batch · CALORIES 189 · FAT 4.5 g · SATURATED FAT 0.5 g · CHOLESTEROL 0 mg · CARBOHYDRATE 35 g · FIBER 5 g · PROTEIN 3 g · SUGARS 7 g · SODIUM 374 mg

Tostones with Peruvian Green Sauce

Tostones are a staple in Latin America and the Caribbean. Also known as *patacones* or fried green plantains, they are typically deep-fried, smashed, then fried again! Using the air fryer reduces the amount of oil needed—just a few spritzes of olive oil and they come out crispy and delicious. You can serve them as a side dish with any meal or as an appetizer with guacamole, ceviche, or one of my favorites, Peruvian green sauce.

1 large green plantain

Kosher salt

¾ teaspoon garlic powder

Olive oil spray

Peruvian Green Sauce
   (recipe follows), for serving

With a sharp knife, trim the ends of the plantain. To make it easier to peel, score a slit along the length of the plantain skin. Cut the plantain crosswise into eight 1-inch pieces and peel the skin off each piece.

In a small bowl, combine 1 cup water with 1 teaspoon salt and the garlic powder.

Preheat the air fryer to 400°F.

Spritz the plantain all over with olive oil and transfer to the air fryer basket. Cook for 6 minutes, shaking halfway, until soft. (For a toaster oven–style air fryer, cook at 375°F; the timing remains the same.) Immediately transfer to a work surface. While they are still hot, use a *tostonera* or the bottom of a glass jar or measuring cup to flatten each piece.

Dip each piece, one at a time, in the seasoned water, then transfer to the work surface (discard the water). Generously spray both sides of the plantain with oil.

Preheat the air fryer to 400°F again.

Working in batches, arrange a single layer of the plantain in the air fryer basket. Cook for about 10 minutes, flipping halfway, until golden and crisp. (For a toaster oven–style air fryer, cook at 375°F for about 8 minutes.) Transfer to a serving

(recipe continues)

PER SERVING: **4 pieces** · CALORIES **108** · FAT **0.5 g** · SATURATED FAT **0 g** · CHOLESTEROL **0 mg** · CARBOHYDRATE **28 g** · FIBER **2 g** · PROTEIN **1 g** · SUGARS **13 g** · SODIUM **564 mg**

dish. While still hot, spray lightly with olive oil and season with ⅛ teaspoon salt. Serve immediately with the green sauce on the side.

skinny scoop A *tostonera* is a wooden (or sometimes plastic) press used to make tostones. If you don't own one, the flat bottom of a glass jar or measuring cup can also be used.

Peruvian Green Sauce

MAKES ABOUT 1⅔ CUPS

I'm seriously obsessed with this sauce! Also known as *ají verde*, it's a spicy, bright-green condiment typically found in Peruvian chicken restaurants in the States. Great on everything from chicken to beans and fish, it's the perfect dip for these crispy tostones. To make this sauce spicier, leave the seeds and ribs in the jalapeños. To make it milder, remove both the seeds and ribs.

2 tablespoons olive oil

¼ cup chopped red onion

½ cup light mayonnaise

2 tablespoons distilled white vinegar

4 teaspoons yellow mustard

½ teaspoon kosher salt

¼ teaspoon freshly ground black pepper

3 jalapeños, seeded (but keep the ribs) and roughly chopped (about 1 cup)

2 cups (2 ounces) chopped fresh cilantro (leaves and stems included)

3 garlic cloves, crushed through a garlic press

In a small skillet, heat 1 teaspoon of the olive oil over medium heat. Add the onion and cook, stirring occasionally, until soft, 3 to 4 minutes.

Transfer the cooked onion to a blender with the remaining 1 tablespoon plus 2 teaspoons oil, the mayonnaise, vinegar, mustard, salt, and black pepper. Add the jalapeños, cilantro, and garlic and blend on high speed until the sauce is smooth and creamy, about 30 seconds. You can store the sauce in a sealed container in the refrigerator for up to 1 week.

PER SERVING: **1 tablespoon** · CALORIES **27** · FAT **2.5 g** · SATURATED FAT **0.5 g** · CHOLESTEROL **2 mg** · CARBOHYDRATE **1 g** · FIBER **0 g** · PROTEIN **0 g** · SUGARS **0.5 g** · SODIUM **60 mg**

Q
V
GF
DF

Breaded Fried Eggplant

Getting your kids to embrace vegetables can be an art form. So naturally, when my daughter Karina discovered her love for breaded, fried eggplant after eating dinner at her friend's house, you better believe I started making it for her all the time! Putting the air fryer to the test, these turned out crisp and delicious—you don't miss all the oil. Karina gave it two thumbs up!

1 large eggplant (about 1½ pounds)

¾ teaspoon kosher salt

Freshly ground black pepper

3 large eggs

1⅔ cups seasoned bread crumbs, whole wheat or gluten-free

Olive oil spray

Marinara sauce, for dipping (optional)

Slice the ends off the eggplant and cut into ¼-inch-thick rounds, 40 to 42 slices. Season both sides with the salt and pepper to taste.

On a shallow plate, beat the eggs with 1 teaspoon water. Place the bread crumbs on another plate. Dip each eggplant slice in the egg, then in the bread crumbs, pressing gently to adhere. Shake off any excess bread crumbs and place on a work surface. Generously spray both sides of the eggplant with oil.

Preheat the air fryer to 380°F.

Working in batches, arrange a single layer of the eggplant in the air fryer basket. Cook for about 8 minutes, flipping halfway, until crisp, golden, and cooked through in the center. (For a toaster oven–style air fryer, cook at 350°F; the timing remains the same.) Serve warm with the marinara, if desired.

skinny scoop The eggplant can be enjoyed as an appetizer or side dish, and it's great plain or with marinara sauce for dipping. If you want to turn this into eggplant Parmesan, you can layer it with cheese and marinara sauce, then bake until melted and heated through.

PER SERVING: **5 pieces** · CALORIES **116** · FAT **3 g** · SATURATED FAT **1 g** · CHOLESTEROL **70 mg** · CARBOHYDRATE **18 g** · FIBER **5 g** · PROTEIN **5 g** · SUGARS **3 g** · SODIUM **515 mg**

DESSERTS

Q
V

Very Berry Mini Pie

I'll never forget the birthday weekend that I spent with my best friends in Tennessee. They surprised me with a homemade berry pie, the way to my heart! This mini pie is made with a combination of four different berries and a touch of orange zest for flavor. I use a store-bought, refrigerated piecrust for speed and place it only on the top to shave calories, so you'll have to serve this with a spoon much like you would a cobbler. Ready to dig in?

Cooking spray

¼ cup raw sugar

2 tablespoons cornstarch

¼ teaspoon vanilla extract

½ teaspoon loosely packed grated orange zest

1 cup halved and sliced strawberries

⅔ cup raspberries

⅔ cup blueberries

⅔ cup blackberries, cut into thirds

1 store-bought refrigerated piecrust

1 large egg

Spray a 5½-inch mini pie dish with cooking spray.

In a medium bowl, combine the sugar, cornstarch, vanilla, and orange zest and mix well. Add the strawberries, raspberries, blueberries, and blackberries and gently toss to combine. Transfer the mixture to the pie dish.

Lay the prepared dough on a work surface, then cut out a 7-inch-diameter round (I use a plate as a guide; it will be about 2¾ ounces of dough). Refrigerate the remaining crust for another recipe. Place the piecrust over the baking dish and crimp the edges to create a seal. Cut 4 slits around the center of the piecrust.

In a small bowl, beat the egg with 1 tablespoon water. Using a pastry brush, brush the top of the crust with the egg wash.

Preheat the air fryer to 350°F.

Place the pie in the air fryer basket. Bake for about 15 minutes, until the crust is golden and the berries are hot and bubbling. (For a toaster oven–style air fryer, place the basket in the lower rack position and bake at 300°F for about 20 minutes.) Let cool for at least 15 minutes before cutting so the filling will thicken. Serve warm.

skinny scoop For the store-bought, refrigerated piecrust, look for the ones that usually come ready to bake in a box.

PER SERVING: **1 slice (about ½ cup)** · CALORIES **213** · FAT **6.5 g** · SATURATED FAT **2.5 g** · CHOLESTEROL **47 mg** · CARBOHYDRATE **37 g** · FIBER **4.5 g** · PROTEIN **3 g** · SUGARS **18 g** · SODIUM **102 mg**

V

Mini Churros

When I told my friends I was coming out with an air fryer cookbook, the one request I kept getting over and over again was for churros. Game on! Growing up, I have great memories of enjoying churros with a cup of hot chocolate—they are just meant for each other. When they're made in the air fryer, they're not just lighter, but the process is safer than deep-frying: no worrying about oil splatters. Now, the only fear is eating one too many!

¼ teaspoon kosher salt

2 tablespoons unsalted butter

3 tablespoons sugar

1 cup all-purpose flour

1 teaspoon vanilla extract

Olive oil spray

½ teaspoon ground cinnamon

skinny scoop: If you don't have a pastry bag with a star tip, use a zip-top plastic bag. Fill the bag with the dough and cut 1¼ inches off the tip of the bottom corner. Pipe the dough as directed, then use a fork to drag the tines over the top of each strip; flip the strip and repeat on the other side.

In a medium pot, combine 1 cup water, the salt, 1 tablespoon of the butter, and 1 tablespoon of the sugar. Bring to a boil over medium-high heat. Once boiling, remove from the heat and add the flour and vanilla. Mix with a wooden spoon until thoroughly combined and a dough-ball forms. Let cool for 5 minutes.

Transfer the dough to a plastic pastry bag fitted with a star tip, pushing the dough into the bottom (see Skinny Scoop). Twist the top of the bag to keep it closed. Pipe 10 (5-inch-long) strips of dough onto a plate or work surface and spray with oil.

Preheat the air fryer to 340°F.

Working in batches, arrange the churros in a single layer in the air fryer basket. Cook for 20 to 22 minutes, flipping halfway, until golden. (For a toaster oven–style air fryer, cook at 275°F for about 26 minutes.)

Meanwhile, melt the remaining tablespoon butter in a small bowl. On a small plate, combine the remaining 2 tablespoons sugar and the cinnamon and mix well.

Remove the churros from the air fryer and transfer to a plate or work surface. Use a pastry brush to lightly brush each with melted butter, then roll in the cinnamon-sugar mixture. Repeat with the remaining churros. (You may have to reheat the butter for the second batch since it will solidify as it cools.) Serve immediately.

PER SERVING: **2 churros** · CALORIES **164** · FAT **5 g** · SATURATED FAT **3 g** · CHOLESTEROL **12 mg** · CARBOHYDRATE **27 g** · FIBER **1 g** · PROTEIN **3 g** · SUGARS **8 g** · SODIUM **57 mg**

Baked Streusel Apples

These baked apples satisfy my craving for apple crumb pie—my favorite kind of pie! They're lighter and quicker to whip up thanks to the air fryer, making them perfect for any night of the week. I serve the apples with a bit of vanilla ice cream for that creamy hot-cold combination I just can't resist, but they're also great with a little whipped cream.

2 large apples (Granny Smith or Gala)

3 tablespoons all-purpose or gluten-free flour

3 tablespoons light brown sugar

1/8 teaspoon ground cinnamon

2 tablespoons cold unsalted butter

Vanilla ice cream, for serving (optional)

Halve the apples through the stem and remove and discard the core and seeds with a small paring knife or spoon.

In a small bowl, combine the flour, brown sugar, and cinnamon. Add the butter and cut it into the flour with a fork until crumbs form. Spoon 2½ tablespoons on top of each apple half.

Preheat the air fryer to 325ºF.

Working in batches, place the apple halves in the air fryer basket. Cook for 25 to 27 minutes, until the apples are soft when pierced through in the center with a paring knife and the crumb topping is golden. (For a toaster oven–style air fryer, cook at 300°F; the timing remains the same.) Serve warm with ice cream, if desired.

PER SERVING: 1/2 baked apple · CALORIES 167 · FAT 6 g · SATURATED FAT 3.5 g · CHOLESTEROL 15 mg · CARBOHYDRATE 29 g · FIBER 2.5 g · PROTEIN 1 g · SUGARS 21 g · SODIUM 5 mg

Q

V

Banana-Apricot Turnovers

With just four ingredients, you can whip up this easy dessert any night of the week in less than 30 minutes. (You just gotta love the convenience of store-bought puff pastry dough!) Feel free to play around with different fruit combinations, such as strawberry preserves and banana or use pie filling instead.

1 (9-ounce) sheet frozen puff pastry dough, thawed

6 teaspoons apricot preserves

3 ripe medium bananas, sliced

1 large egg, beaten

Cut the puff pastry into 6 rectangles. Using a rolling pin, roll each piece out into a 5-inch square.

Place a square of puff pastry on a work surface with the points facing top and bottom like a diamond. Spoon 1 teaspoon of the apricot preserves on the bottom half. Spread evenly on the bottom only, leaving a ½-inch border from the edge. Top the apricot with half of one banana. Brush the edges of the pastry square with some of the beaten egg. Fold the top corner over to form a triangle. Using a fork, seal the edges all around. Brush the top with more egg. Repeat with the remaining puff pastry, apricot preserves, bananas, and egg.

Preheat the air fryer to 350°F.

Working in batches, place the turnovers in the air fryer basket. Cook for about 10 minutes, flipping halfway, until the pastry is golden and puffed. (For a toaster oven–style air fryer, cook at 300°F for about 6 minutes.) Let cool a few minutes before serving.

PER SERVING: **1 turnover** · CALORIES **315** · FAT **17 g** · SATURATED FAT **4.5 g** · CHOLESTEROL **31 mg** · CARBOHYDRATE **37 g** · FIBER **2 g** · PROTEIN **5 g** · SUGARS **11 g** · SODIUM **121 mg**

SERVES
4

Q
V
GF
DF

Roasted Peaches with Ice Cream

Peaches and cream is one of the most quintessential desserts. The classic pairing is phenomenal with sweet, perfectly ripe, summer peaches. Baked in the air fryer until warm and golden, topped with a little vanilla ice cream or frozen yogurt, this dessert couldn't get any easier!

4 peaches, halved and pitted

1 cup vanilla ice cream, frozen yogurt, or dairy-free ice cream

2 tablespoons slivered almonds

4 sprigs spearmint, for garnish

Preheat the air fryer to 375°F.

Working in batches, arrange a single layer of peach halves cut sides up in the air fryer basket. Cook for about 10 minutes, until the peaches are soft and golden brown on top. (For a toaster oven–style air fryer, the temperature remains the same; cook for about 8 minutes.)

Divide the peaches among 4 serving bowls. Place 2-tablespoon scoops of ice cream in the center of each peach half. Top with the slivered almonds and mint and serve immediately.

PER SERVING: **2 halves** · CALORIES **149** · FAT **6 g** · SATURATED FAT **2.5 g** · CHOLESTEROL **15 mg** · CARBOHYDRATE **23 g** · FIBER **3 g** · PROTEIN **3 g** · SUGARS **20 g** · SODIUM **27 mg**

CONVENTIONAL OVEN COOKING CHART

If you want to make the recipes in this book in your conventional oven instead of an air fryer, I've provided cook times below to use for the oven. Keep in mind that the results won't be as crisp as they would be if they were cooked in the air fryer, but following this guide should get you close. All recipes are cooked on a sheet pan lightly sprayed with oil, unless noted otherwise.

RECIPE	PAGE NUMBER	OVEN TEMPERATURE	COOK TIME
Veggie-Leek and Cheese Frittata	15	375°F	35 minutes (I used a 6-inch cake pan)
Everything-but-the-Bagel Breakfast Pockets	16	425°F	16 to 18 minutes, flipping halfway (on center rack)
PB&J Oatmeal Bake with Bananas and Blueberries	18	350°F	40 minutes
Home Fries with Onions and Peppers	19	375°F	25 to 30 minutes
Homemade Bagels	20	375°F	25 minutes (on the top rack)
Cinnamon Rolls with Cream Cheese Icing	23	350°F	20 to 25 minutes
Breakfast Turkey Sausage	25	Broil on high	4 to 5 minutes, flipping halfway
Petite Spiced Pumpkin Bread	26	350°F	45 minutes, rotating halfway
Blueberry-Lemon Yogurt Muffins	29	375°F	16 to 18 minutes
Buffalo Wings with Blue Cheese Dip	32	425°F	45 minutes, flipping halfway
Chicken-Vegetable Spring Rolls	35	400°F	12 to 16 minutes, flipping halfway
Bacon-Wrapped Cheesy Jalapeño Poppers	36	400°F	16 to 18 minutes
Crab and Cream Cheese Wontons	39	400°F	10 to 12 minutes, flipping halfway (generously spray sheet pan with oil)
Baked Clam Dip	40	350°F	30 minutes, top with Parmesan and paprika, then bake 3 to 4 minutes more
Cheesy Crab-Stuffed Mushrooms	43	400°F	20 to 22 minutes
Ahi Poke Wonton Cups	44	300°F	14 to 15 minutes (for the cups)
Homemade Chips and Salsa	46	425°F	7 to 8 minutes, flipping halfway
Tomatillo Salsa Verde	48	Broil on high	6 to 8 minutes, flipping halfway (for the tomatillos)
Devils on Horseback	49	425°F	12 to 14 minutes, flipping halfway
Loaded Zucchini Skins	51	400°F for bacon; 375°F for zucchini	Cook the bacon for 10 minutes, flipping halfway. Cook the zucchini for 8 to 10 minutes, add the cheese and bacon, and cook for 2 to 3 minutes more.
Cauliflower Rice Arancini	52	425°F	25 minutes
Crispy Za'atar Chickpeas	55	375°F	35 to 45 minutes, shaking every 10 minutes
Garlic Knots	56	375°F	18 minutes (in top third of oven)
Fried Pickle Chips with Cajun Buttermilk Ranch	59	450°F	15 minutes, flipping halfway

BREAKFAST

APPETIZERS & SNACKS

RECIPE	PAGE NUMBER	OVEN TEMPERATURE	COOK TIME
POULTRY			
Chicken Parmesan Caprese	64	425°F	8 minutes, flipping halfway, then add cheese and tomatoes and bake 3 to 4 minutes more
Parmesan-Crusted Turkey Cutlets with Arugula Salad	64	425°F	12 to 14 minutes, flipping halfway
Herbed Cornish Hen for Two	65	375°F	1 hour (in a roasting rack set in a roasting pan)
Adobo-Rubbed Chicken with Avocado Salsa	68	425°F	15 to 16 minutes, flipping halfway
Naked Seasoned Chicken Tenders	69	400°F	40 to 50 minutes, flipping halfway
Pickle-Brined Chicken Tenders	70	425°F	8 to 10 minutes, flip, then 6 minutes more (in lower third of oven)
Asian Turkey Meatballs with Hoisin Sauce	73	425°F	18 to 20 minutes, flipping halfway
Chicken Piccata	74	425°F	8 minutes, flipping halfway
Cornflake-Crusted "Fried" Chicken with Romaine Slaw	76	400°F	40 to 45 minutes, flipping halfway
Spiced Yogurt-Marinated Chicken Thighs with Blistered Vegetables	78	425°F	30 minutes, then broil on high for 4 to 5 minutes (on the second rack from the top)
Cheesy Green Chile–Chicken Chimichangas	80	400°F	18 to 20 minutes
Chicken Cordon Bleu	82	450°F	25 minutes
Fiesta Turkey Meatloaves	83	400°F	12 minutes, add glaze, then 12 minutes more
BEEF, PORK & LAMB			
Low-Carb Cheeseburger Sliders with Special Sauce	86	Broil on high	4 minutes, flipping halfway, for medium doneness (on top rack)
Roast Beef with Horseradish-Chive Cream	89	350°F	1 hour and 10 minutes (for medium rare)
Carne Asada Salad	90	Broil on high	6 minutes, flipping halfway (for medium to medium rare; on top rack)
Soy-Sesame Marinated Flank Steak	91	Broil on high	8 minutes (for medium rare) or 10 minutes (for medium), flipping halfway (on top rack)
Korean Pork Lettuce Wraps	92	Broil on high	5 to 6 minutes, flipping halfway (on top rack)
Meat Lovers' Pizza-Stuffed Peppers	93	Broil on high for sausage; 375°F for peppers	Broil sausage for 7 to 8 minutes, flipping halfway. Bake peppers for 16 to 18 minutes at 375°F. Stuff peppers and bake 10 to 12 minutes more.
Breaded Pork Cutlets with Avocado, Tomatoes, and Lime	94	425°F	12 to 14 minutes, flipping halfway
Apple-Stuffed Pork Chops	97	400°F	10 minutes, flip and baste, then 10 minutes more (generously spray sheet pan with oil)
Five-Spice Glazed Lamb Chops	98	Broil on high	8 minutes, flipping halfway

RECIPE	PAGE NUMBER	OVEN TEMPERATURE	COOK TIME
SEAFOOD			
Crispy Coconut Shrimp with Sweet Chili Mayo	102	425°F	15 to 18 minutes, flipping halfway
Shrimp Empanadas	105	400°F	18 minutes
Lemony Shrimp and Zucchini with Mint	106	400°F	10 minutes for zucchini only, add shrimp, and bake 8 minutes more
Tortilla Shrimp Tacos with Cilantro-Lime Slaw	107	425°F	15 to 18 minutes, flipping halfway
Crab Cake Sandwiches with Cajun Mayo	108	400°F	20 minutes
Blackened Salmon with Cucumber-Avocado Salsa	111	450°F	10 to 12 minutes, flipping halfway
Roasted Fish with Lemon-Almond Crumbs	112	425°F	10 to 12 minutes
Fish Croquettes with Lemon-Dill Aioli	113	400°F	16 to 18 minutes, flipping halfway
Salmon Burgers with Lemon-Caper Rémoulade	114	Broil on high	8 minutes, flipping halfway
VEGETABLE MAINS & SIDES			
Tomato, Spinach, and Feta Stuffed Portobellos	118	400°F	18 to 20 minutes
Sesame-Crusted Teriyaki Tofu "Steaks"	121	350°F	30 minutes, flipping halfway (generously spray sheet pan with oil)
Buffalo Cauliflower Nuggets	122	450°F	20 minutes
Mexican Street Corn	124	Broil on high	7 to 8 minutes, flipping 4 or 5 times
Sugar and Spice Acorn Squash	125	350°F	In a baking dish filled with ¼ cup water, cover and bake for 50 minutes. Uncover and bake 10 minutes more.
Brussels Sprouts with Bacon	127	425°F	40 minutes, flipping halfway
Charred Sesame Green Beans	128	425°F	15 minutes, flipping halfway
Bacon-Wrapped Asparagus Bundles	131	450°F	10 to 12 minutes
French Fries	132	425°F	20 minutes, flipping halfway
Cheddar Broccoli Gratin	135	350°F	22 to 25 minutes
Crispy Onion Rings	136	400°F	20 minutes, flipping halfway
Perfectly Baked Potatoes with Yogurt and Chives	137	350°F	1 hour and 15 minutes (directly on oven rack)
Crispy Sweet Potato Fries	138	425°F	24 to 30 minutes, flipping halfway
Tostones with Peruvian Green Sauce	141	425°F	Microwave whole plantain until soft in center, 3 to 3½ minutes. Bake smashed plantain 18 to 20 minutes, flipping halfway.
Breaded Fried Eggplant	143	450°F	8 to 9 minutes
DESSERTS			
Very Berry Mini Pie	146	400°F	34 to 36 minutes
Mini Churros	149	350°F	30 to 35 minutes, flipping halfway
Baked Streusel Apples	150	350°F	46 to 50 minutes
Banana-Apricot Turnovers	153	400°F	16 to 20 minutes
Roasted Peaches with Ice Cream	154	400°F	18 to 20 minutes (in a baking dish)

INDEX

Note: Page references in *italics* indicate photographs.

ACKNOWLEDGMENTS

A heartfelt thank-you to the whole team who helped put this air fryer cookbook together.

First off, the biggest thank-you to the Skinnytaste family and to my dedicated fans—you are my "why."

To my family, who are always so supportive and gladly willing to act as my taste testers.

As always, working with my friend Heather K. Jones, R.D., on this fourth cookbook—it's hard to believe!—has been a joy. Your positive energy makes this whole process less stressful. Thank you for always keeping me calm. And to her team, Danielle Hazard, Donna Fennessy, and Jackie Price, for paying attention to all the details.

To my aunt Ligia Caldas, who keeps me organized and chops veggies like a pro. Thank you for being my right hand!

To my brilliant, fearless agent, Janis Donnaud, I am so glad to always have you in my corner!

To the stellar team at Clarkson Potter: Doris Cooper, Jenn Sit, Carly Gorga, Stephanie Davis, Erica Gelbard, Stephanie Huntwork, Patricia Shaw, Derek Gullino, and Marysarah Quinn: I love working with you all.

I am so grateful for my talented photographer, Aubrie Pick, and her incredible team, including first assistant Tatum Mangus, food stylist Vivian Lui, food stylist assistants Cybelle Tondu and Brett Regot, and prop stylist Maeve Sheridan.

And last but not least, to all my girlfriends: thank you for always supporting me on this fun and crazy ride!

Published in the United States by Clarkson Potter/Publishers, an imprint of the Crown Publishing Group, a division of Penguin Random House LLC, New York.
crownpublishing.com
clarksonpotter.com

CLARKSON POTTER is a trademark and POTTER with colophon is a registered trademark of Penguin Random House LLC.

Skinnytaste™ is a trademark of Skinnytaste, Inc.

Library of Congress Cataloging-in-Publication Data
Names: Homolka, Gina, author. | Jones, Heather K., author.
Title: The skinnytaste air fryer cookbook : the 75 best healthy recipes
    for your air fryer / Gina Homolka with Heather K. Jones.
Description: First edition. | New York : Clarkson Potter/Publishers, 2019. |
    Includes bibliographical references and index.
Identifiers: LCCN 2018060753| ISBN 9781984825643
    (hardcover ; alk. paper) |
    ISBN 9781984825650 (ebook : alk. paper)
Subjects: LCSH: Hot air frying. | LCGFT: Cookbooks.
Classification: LCC TX689 .H66 2019 | DDC 641.7/7--dc23 LC
    record available at https://lccn.loc.gov/2018060753

ISBN 978-1-9848-2564-3
Ebook ISBN 978-1-9848-2565-0

Printed in the United States of America

Photographs by Aubrie Pick
Book and cover design by Stephanie Huntwork

10 9 8 7 6 5 4 3 2 1

First Edition